GROUNDBREAKER
CRABTREE BIOGRAPHIES

Steve Jobs

VISIONARY ENTREPRENEUR
OF THE DIGITAL AGE

By Jude Isabella and Matt J. Simmons

Crabtree Publishing Company
www.crabtreebooks.com

Crabtree Publishing Company
www.crabtreebooks.com

Authors: Jude Isabella and Matt J. Simmons
Publishing plan research and development:
  Reagan Miller
Project coordinator: Mark Sachner,
  Water Buffalo Books
Editors: Mark Sachner, Lynn Peppas
Proofreader: Wendy Scavuzzo
Indexer: Gini Holland
Editorial director: Kathy Middleton
Photo researcher: Water Buffalo Books
Designer: Westgraphix/Tammy West
Production and print coordinator: Margaret Amy Salter
Production: Kim Richardson
Prepress technician: Margaret Amy Salter

Written, developed, and produced by Water Buffalo Books

Photographs and reproductions:
Alamy: dominic dibbs: p. 8 (left). **Associated Press:** cover (right).
Corbis: DB Apple/dpa/Corbis: p. 44; Ed Kashi/VII/Corbis:
pp. 49 (left), 60, 62; Frederic Larson/San Francisco Chronicle/
Corbis: p. 76; Reuters/CORBIS: p. 83; George Steinmetz/Corbis:
p. 103. **Getty Images:** Bloomberg via Getty Images: p. 30; Hulton
Archive/Getty Images: pp. 34, 66; Time & Life Pictures/Getty
Images: p. 51; Archive Photos/Getty Images: p. 57. **iStockphoto:**
Scott Hirko: cover (left). **Public domain:** pp. 6 (left), 11 (all), 36, 45
(bottom), 47, 78, 79 (top, middle), 97. **Mark Sachner:** p. 89 (bottom).
Shutterstock: Featureflash: pp. 1, 5, 38, 59, 77; Annette Shaff: pp. 7,
20, 50; null7711: pp. 14, 32, 46, 92; anuphadit: p. 28; Bocman1973:
p. 41 (left); bioraven: p. 43; IVY PHOTOS: p. 54; Jaguar PS: pp. 63;
catwalker: p. 85 (all); Burlingham : p. 87; Denys Prykhodov: p.
100. **Tammy West:** p. 98 (bottom). **Wikipedia Creative Commons:**
p. 74; Erik Pitti: p. 4; afrank99: p. 8 (right); Argonne National
Laboratory: p. 9; Rico Shen: p. 12; Joi Ito: p. 17; jjron/John O'Neill:
p. 18 (left); Chris Rand: p. 18 (top right); madmaxmarchhare: p. 18
(bottom right); Maya Visvanathan: p. 22; OSU Special Collections
& Archives: Commons @ Flickr Commons: p. 24 (left); Michael: p.
24 (right); Ysbrand Cosijn: p. 26; mylerdude: p. 33; Rob Bouden: p.
37; John crane 59: p. 41 (right); Rama: p. 45 (top); Lisa Brennan-Jobs,
Lisa Jobs: p. 49 (right); Kees de Vos: p. 55; CC-BY-SA: p. 65; www.
allaboutapple.com: p. 69; Gobierno de Chile: p. 67; Casey Fleser:
p. 71; Mikhail (Vokabre) Shcherbakov: p. 73; Benjamin5lu: p. 79
(bottom); Gary Cohen: p. 80; Silvio Tanaka: p. 81; Chris Schuepp:
p. 88; Doudoulolita: p. 89 (top left); Jimmy Flink: p. 89 (top right);
Davemn: p. 90; 1DmkIIN: p. 94; Mikepanhu: p. 95 (both); Matthew
Yohe: p. 96; matt buchanan: p. 98 (top); Jeremy Keith: p. 99; Mathieu
Thouvenin: p. 101.

Publisher's note:
All quotations in this book come from original sources and contain the
spelling and grammatical inconsistencies of the original text. Some of the
quotations may also contain terms that are no longer in use and may be
considered inappropriate or offensive. The use of such terms is for the
sake of preserving the historical and literary accuracy of the sources and
should not be seen as encouraging or endorsing the use of such terms
today.

Cover: Background: A Macintosh computer like the one presented
with great fanfare by Steve Jobs in 1984. Foreground: Steve introduces
the MacBook Air, a new family of super-thin, ultraportable notebook
computers, at a Macworld convention in 2008. The Mac, which has
become the signature brand of Apple Inc., is loved by many Mac fans
as much for its style as for its computing capabilities.

Library and Archives Canada Cataloguing in Publication

Isabella, Jude, author
    Steve Jobs : visionary entrepreneur of the digital
age / Jude Isabella and Matt J. Simmons.

(Crabtree groundbreaker biographies)
Includes index.
Issued in print and electronic formats.
ISBN 978-0-7787-1189-6 (bound).--ISBN 978-0-7787-1191-9 (pbk.).
--ISBN 978-1-4271-8938-7 (pdf).--ISBN 978-1-4271-8936-3 (html)

    1. Jobs, Steve, 1955-2011--Juvenile literature. 2. Apple
Computer, Inc.--History--Juvenile literature. 3. Computer
engineers--United States--Biography--Juvenile literature. 4.
Businesspeople--United States--Biography--Juvenile literature.
I. Simmons, Matt J., 1980-, author II. Title. III. Series: Crabtree
groundbreaker biographies.

QA76.2.J63I73 2014   j621.39092   C2013-907482-1
                                            C2013-907483-X

Library of Congress Cataloging-in-Publication Data

Isabella, Jude.
    Steve Jobs : visionary entrepreneur of the digital age / by Jude
Isabella and Matt J. Simmons.
        pages cm. -- (Crabtree groundbreaker biographies)
    Includes index.
    ISBN 978-0-7787-1189-6 (reinforced library binding) -- ISBN
978-0-7787-1191-9 (pbk.) -- ISBN 978-1-4271-8938-7 (electronic pdf)
-- ISBN 978-1-4271-8936-3 (electronic html)
    1. Jobs, Steve, 1955-2011. 2. Computer industry--United States-
-Biography. 3. Businesspeople--United States--Biography. 4.
Computer engineers--United States--Biography. I. Simmons, Matt
J. II. Title.

HD9696.2.U62J6358 2014
338.7'61004092--dc23
[B]
                                            2013042828

Crabtree Publishing Company
www.crabtreebooks.com   1-800-387-7650

Printed in Canada/012014/BF20131120

**Published
in Canada
Crabtree Publishing**
616 Welland Ave.
St. Catharines, Ontario
L2M 5V6

**Published in
the United States
Crabtree Publishing**
PMB 59051
350 Fifth Ave., 59th Floor
New York, NY 10118

**Published in the
United Kingdom
Crabtree Publishing**
Maritime House
Basin Road North, Hove
BN41 1WR

**Published
in Australia
Crabtree Publishing**
3 Charles Street
Coburg North
VIC, 3058

Contents

English
French
German
Italian
Spanish
Portugue
Polish
Dutch

Steve Jobs discusses the foreign-language features of the iPhone at an Apple event in 2008. Steve's talks, which became known as "Stevenotes," were eagerly anticipated at these events by the Mac faithful and did much to stir up enthusiasm for Apple products.

Chapter 1
Giving the People What They Want

January 24, 1984. More than 2,500 people sit in a dark auditorium, facing a large blank screen at a community college in Cupertino, California. Steve Jobs, co-founder of Apple Computer, Inc. (today known simply as Apple Inc.), has just finished telling them a story. It is a story about how one big corporation wants to control the computer industry. This big corporation, called IBM (International Business Machines), wants to dominate the information age, Jobs says. He compares IBM with Big Brother, a figure representing a shadowy organization that controls people's lives in the famous book *1984* by George Orwell. The audience waits in the darkness.

1984, Apple-Style

Creeping black, white, and gray images flicker across the screen. A line of bald human drones—maybe men, maybe women—now appears on the screen, marching toward the viewers. A menacing voice can be heard, babbling on and on about how everything needs to be uniform, the same. Then the camera catches a woman running. She has short blond hair, and she's dressed in a white tank top and socks, bright red shorts and sneakers. She sprints down a hallway, her hands grasping the handle of a sledgehammer.

Steve Jobs at the 2001 world premiere of the Disney/Pixar movie Monsters, Inc., *in Hollywood. After Steve left Apple in 1985, he became an investor in Pixar Animation Studios, home of such computer-animated hits as* Finding Nemo, The Incredibles, *and the* Toy Story, Cars, *and* Monsters, Inc. *movies.*

The camera cuts back to the marching gray drones, then to the menacing voice—a man's face on a video screen is lecturing to more gray drones. It's Big Brother. The woman sprints toward the video screen, chased by gray police dressed in riot gear. They're getting closer. The woman stops. She twirls, swinging the sledgehammer around like an Olympic athlete. She lets go, and the sledgehammer sails through the air. It hits the video screen, which explodes in a burst of wind, light, and smoke. The gray drones' mouths open. They're free! The image shifts. A rainbow-colored apple, with a bite taken out of it, pops onto the screen following this message:

On January 24th,
Apple Computer will introduce Macintosh.
And you'll see why 1984 won't be like "1984."

The crowd reacts to the Apple commercial with cheers and whoops. Steve loves it. He has given the people what they want, a story and a product that reflect who they are.

The Revolutionary Apple

When the audience quiets down, Steve strolls across the stage into a spotlight and next to a bag resting on a table. Inside is something revolutionary. Steve looks like a magician as he unzips the bag and lifts out a light-colored plastic object with a small screen. He fishes a plastic diskette out of his left breast pocket and holds it out as though for show-and-tell. People clap and laugh as Steve slips the disk into a slot at the front of the box, and the screen lights up. To music from the movie *Chariots of Fire*, the letters M-A-C-I-N-T-O-S-H roll by. Underneath, an invisible hand writes, "Insanely great!"

There is more to come. Images of what the Mac can do burst onto the screen. Art objects and computer "tool" icons. A drop-down menu bar at the top of the screen. Different fonts. An image of Steve Jobs and a thought bubble with a Mac inside. A chess game with pieces out of *Alice in Wonderland*.

There is still more to come. Steve speaks again: "We've done a lot of talking about Macintosh recently. But today, for the first time ever, I'd like to let Macintosh speak for itself." Steve clicks on a mouse next to the computer.

"Hello, I'm Macintosh," the computer says as the text appears on the screen. "It sure is great to get out of that bag." The computer continues in a deep electronic voice:

"Unaccustomed as I am to public speaking, I'd like to share with you a maxim I thought of the first time I met an IBM mainframe: NEVER TRUST A COMPUTER YOU CAN'T LIFT. [The audience laughs.] Obviously, I can talk. But right now I'd like to sit back and listen. So it is with considerable pride that I introduce a man who's been like a father to me … STEVE JOBS."

Twenty-eight-year-old Steve Jobs poses with his pride and joy—the original Apple Macintosh computer, launched in January 1984. Inset: This diskette is similar to the one Steve inserted into the Mac's hard drive following his presentation of Apple's "1984" commercial. At the time, saving data onto small diskettes was the only way to move files from one personal computer to another.

Macintosh wows the audience. The audience claps, cheers, and whistles. They stomp their feet and pump their fists in the air. Steve beams. He has handed them the future. After Macintosh, nothing about making, designing, or using personal computers—the way they work, how they look, the things they can do, where they can be used—will ever be same.

Born at the Right Time

Steve Jobs was born in 1955, in the middle of the post-World War II baby boom. It was a crossroads in time, a point 10 years after the war ended in 1945 and 10 years before the beginning of hippie music festivals in 1965. These events—World War II and the youth culture of the 1960s—created a framework for changes in technology and society that have shaped the way we live today.

Steve was also physically at the crossroads of changes in technology and society. Geographically, California was ground zero for the technological and social revolutions that would reshape the second half of the 20th century. This is where Apple was founded and where Steve grew up—in the Santa Clara Valley, close to San Francisco, the city of his birth.

SIMON, THE FIRST

A mathematician gave the world the first personal computer almost 30 years before Apple became a company. Edmund Berkeley called his machine Simon, after the Simple Simon character in "Mother Goose" nursery rhymes.

Berkeley explained how to build Simon in his 1949 book *Giant Brains, or Machines That Think*. Two electrical engineering students and a mechanic helped him build Simon at a total cost of $600. Simon could perform nine operations, including addition, subtraction, and "greater than." Simon was also portable, and could be carried in one hand. Simon never had a splashy stage introduction like the one Steve Jobs gave Macintosh, but it did appear on the cover of *Scientific American* magazine.

Simon was never a computer that could be bought in an electronics store. Berkeley made Simon available by selling instructions for how to build it. He sold over 500 plans. Berkeley's ultimate goal was to educate people about the new electronic technology of computers by offering the kit as a hands-on experience of building one.

Back in the 1950s, the machine shown here was pretty much what most people thought of when they heard the word "computer." Simon, the first personal computer, would have been lost in a photograph like this!

The Cold War and Technological Change

World War II had brought high-tech industry to the Santa Clara Valley. The nearby Port of San Francisco was a gateway to supplying equipment to the U.S. military based in and around the Pacific Ocean. The federal government had invested in aerospace and electronics research, including an electronics lab at nearby Stanford University, which was based in Palo Alto near Steve's hometown of Los Altos.

The military continued investing in research throughout much of Steve's life. Post-World War II tensions between the United States and communist nations such as the former Soviet Union brought about what was known as the Cold War. The Cold War was not fought on a battlefield. Rather, it was a struggle for superiority in many areas, including technology. It sent satellites and humans into space and created a nuclear weapons race— and the computing power to make it all work. During this time, engineers for big electronics companies, such as Hewlett-Packard, Intel, and Xerox, fueled all that computing power.

Youth Movement and Social Change

In nearby San Francisco, a youth movement was taking off, helping to spur social change. Many baby boomers grew up as members of this movement. They were known by many names, such as the youth subculture or the counterculture, based on their being "counter to," or opposed to, mainstream society. Many members of this movement simply called themselves hippies.

"I grew up in the apricot orchards that later became known as Silicon Valley, and was lucky enough to have my young spirit infused with the social and artistic revolution of the day called rock and roll. It has never left me."

Steve Jobs

Born in 1955, Steve Jobs came into the world at the height of the post-World War II baby boom. His birth placed him at the center of two decades of incredible change. This period started with the end of World War II in 1945, led to both economic prosperity and the so-called Cold War against the Soviet Union, and culminated in a time marked by both space-age technology and cultural changes that most of us know simply as "the sixties."

Right: Two images from post-World War II America during the 1950s, around the time Steve Jobs was born. One of them shows Americans gathered around their TV during a time of, for some, economic prosperity. On a darker note, a comic book graphically envisions an assault on that American way of life during an imagined attack by communists during the Cold War.

Below: Demonstrators against the Vietnam War are met by military police during a 1967 march in Washington, DC. A young protester offers one of the officers a flower as a symbol of peace. The photo is considered a classic image of the 1960s counterculture.

Young people generally tend to embrace change more easily and question the status quo, or the way things are in politics and society, more often than older people. In the 1960s, hippies took this tendency even further. They grew their hair longer, wore clothing that was out of the ordinary, and questioned society and the government through protest, books, and music. Their actions highlighted environmental pollution, the social injustices faced by women and minorities, and the morality of the Vietnam War.

Steve soaked up the booming electronic research going on in Palo Alto. And like many baby boomers, he also embraced the hippie culture that grew out of nearby San Francisco and spread across the nation.

By the early 1970s, the protests begun in the 1960s had led to change. New laws protected people from discrimination and the environment from polluters. The U.S. government also abandoned the Vietnam War effort. By 1973, the year Steve turned 18, the remaining soldiers in Southeast Asia came home.

That same year, the first handheld cellular telephone call was made.

Two New Worlds in One

Steve embraced two worlds. One included the thought-provoking ideas of the hippie movement; the other, the high-tech breakthroughs of engineers.

In 2007, Martin Cooper, the "father of the cell phone," reenacts a historic event he created in 1973—the first call on a handheld cell phone.

CREATIVITY: WE KNOW IT WHEN WE SEE IT

Creativity is a difficult quality to define, but we know that Steve Jobs had it. When we think of people who are creative, artists, dancers, composers, writers, or musicians usually come to mind. So do master chefs, fashion designers, and filmmakers. Just about anyone can be creative, however, in whatever they do. Certainly, businesspersons, scientists, inventors, mathematicians, engineers, teachers, and doctors can be just as creative in their fields as artists are in theirs.

To be creative means making connections, seeing patterns, and coming up with a new idea or improving an old one. Most creative people are open to new experiences, and they love to think. A new experience can change the way we see the world.

As Steve Jobs said after he left Apple, "Creativity is just connecting things... [Creative people] connect experiences they've had and synthesize [create by combining] new things. And the reason they [are] able to do that [is] that they've had more experiences or they have thought more about their experiences than other people."

Thinking creatively is not always a solo activity. It is often social. When someone offers an idea to a group of thoughtful people, the idea might change, grow, and become better. Steve thrived among others who shared his vision and whose talents he felt complemented his own. He was an inspired and inspiring leader in the development of ideas and products for an information age that he had helped shape.

Steve's creative personality had many sides to it, and they often seemed to be in play at once. For those who lived and worked with him, simply being in the presence of this charming charismatic man was often its own reward. One of his gifts was a style that seemed reassuring in its laid-back, easygoing quality. He was also driven and could be ruthless in his demands for the same kind of excellence from others that he expected of himself. As easily given to harsh and callous criticism as to lavish praise, he was what many considered a "difficult" guy to work with.

And yet, while Steve was the face of Apple, his openness to new experiences and his interactions with other creative people helped turn wildly original ideas into wildly popular products.

He came to understand that no matter who we are, each of us is capable of changing the world. With his quick mind and creativity, an ability to act on an idea, and the kind of brashness known as *chutzpah*, Steve combined the two worlds to create Apple in 1977. Apple became a company that would be at the forefront of societal change, most often when Steve was its leader.

Six-year-olds might have bought into the idea of home computers, but not their moms and dads.

Driving Through Failure on the Road to Success

Apple would transform the computer, movie, music, communications, and retail industries. Yet Steve's path was anything but straightforward. Before achieving the success of his later years, he would experience failure in the very company he had created.

In 1985, a little more than a year after Steve had unveiled the Macintosh, the computer industry in general and Apple in particular were in trouble. That year, at the age of just 30 years, Steve was already worth millions of dollars. He received the kind of mail that people who change the world get. One letter, from a six-and-a-half-year-old boy, read as follows:

"Dear Mr. Jobs, I was doing a crossword puzzle and a clue was 'As American as apple blank.' I thought the answer was 'computer,' but my mom said it was 'pie.'"

Six-year-olds might have bought into the idea of home computers, but not their moms and dads. Macintosh wowed ordinary people, but not many were buying them, and Apple had lost millions of dollars trying to sell computers into homes.

Big companies were shutting down manufacturing plants, and upstart Apple was in trouble, its business sliding faster than a marshmallow off a roasting stick. Apple was losing in the computer market to IBM, in part because business people thought Apple computers didn't look real. "They look a little bit like toys," one businessperson told television reporters. She trusted IBM.

Businesses bought computers, and Apple decided it should get more serious about selling computers to businesses. But it faced the reputation of being too flaky and laid back. Apple had lost its shine. So in 1985, just a year after Steve Jobs had transformed the computer industry with his unveiling of the Macintosh, Apple's board of directors kicked him off of Apple's Macintosh project team. Steve wound up leaving Apple, looking like a failure. He was no longer part of the company he had started with a friend when he was just 21 years old. He had poured himself into Apple from the start, then the Macintosh computer project. What would he do with himself now?

Steve was still full of ideas. How would he make them real?

"Older people sit down and ask, 'What is it?' but the boy asks, 'What can I do with it?'"

Steve Jobs, on giving a Macintosh to a boy for his ninth birthday in 1985

Chapter 2
Early Life and Education

In San Francisco on February 24, 1955, 23-year-old college graduate student Joanne Schieble gave birth to a baby boy. She and the baby's father Abdulfattah John Jandali weren't married, and Joanne gave up the baby for adoption. She had one condition for any prospective adoptive parents: They had to be college graduates.

The Parents: Biological and Adoptive

Joanne had grown up in rural Wisconsin. Her father, who was from Germany and had settled in the Green Bay area with his wife and family, was a strict man. When Joanne was younger, she had fallen in love with an artist. Her father disapproved of the match because the artist wasn't Catholic. Later, as a graduate student at the University of Wisconsin in Madison, Joanne again became involved with a man of another faith, and again she faced her father's disapproval.

A video image of Steve Jobs on a screen during a live appearance at a high-tech conference in 2007. Over the years, photos and clips of Steve in front of large audiences, usually with a screen providing larger-than-life images of him showing off new products, became nearly as commonplace as the products themselves.

A tale of three cities in the life of Steve Jobs's biological mother, Joanne Schieble. Clockwise from above, top: a view of Green Bay, Wisconsin, the city to which Joanne's father had moved when he came to America from Germany, and the area where Joanne was raised; a view in Madison of the Wisconsin State Capitol, as seen from a hillside on the campus of the University of Wisconsin, where Joanne met Steve's biological father Abdulfattah John Jandali; and a view of Fisherman's Wharf in San Francisco, the city where Joanne gave birth to Steve, and the area near where Steve was raised by Paul and Clara Jobs.

That man was Abdulfattah, and he was also a student in Madison. Abdulfattah, who was Muslim, came from a wealthy family in Syria and was in the United States to study. Joanne traveled with Abdulfattah to the Middle East in 1954, staying for a couple of months with his family in Homs, Syria. When they arrived back in Wisconsin, Joanne discovered that she was pregnant. The couple wanted to get married, but Joanne knew her father, who was dying, would never approve. Rather than go against her father's wishes, Joanne decided not to marry.

In the 1950s, it was not as socially acceptable for unmarried women to have children and raise them as it is today, so Joanne felt she needed to give up her baby for adoption. She went to San Francisco, where she met with a doctor who helped young women who were pregnant and looking to have their babies adopted. The doctor delivered the healthy baby boy and quietly arranged for him to be adopted by a lawyer and his wife.

The prospective parents had wanted a little girl, and they backed out of the adoption when they learned that Joanne had given birth to a boy. It was instead arranged for the baby to be adopted by a different couple—Paul Jobs, who was an auto mechanic, and Clara Jobs, who was a bookkeeper. At first, Joanne refused to sign the adoption papers. Neither Paul nor Clara had graduated from college, but that wasn't the only reason Joanne was stalling. She knew her father was dying and thought, if she waited, she could marry Abdulfattah and take back their baby.

After a few weeks, despite her misgivings, Joanne gave in. She signed the adoption papers, on the condition that the adoptive parents start an educational fund for the baby so he could go to college. Paul and Clara promised to save money for the boy's education.

Baby Steven Paul Jobs

Not long after giving up her baby, Joanne's father died, and she married Abdulfattah. But the baby, named Steven Paul Jobs, had other parents now, parents who were quite different from Joanne and Abdulfattah.

Like Joanne, Paul Jobs was born and raised on a dairy farm in rural Wisconsin, but he had dropped out of high school. He wandered the Midwest working as a mechanic, eventually signing up for the U.S. Coast Guard when he was 19 years old. During World War II, Paul served in Italy.

Clara Hagopian was born in New Jersey. She was the child of parents who had fled to America when the Ottoman Empire (present-day Turkey) invaded their homeland of Armenia earlier in the 20th century. The family moved to San Francisco when Clara was a child. Clara married young. Her first husband was killed in World War II.

In 1945, the war was over, and Paul's ship ended its service in San Francisco. The young mechanic made a bet with his friends that within two weeks he would meet the woman he would marry. He met Clara soon after, and 10 days later they were engaged.

The young married couple moved to Wisconsin to live with Paul's parents for a while before Paul landed a mechanic's job with a big agricultural company in Indiana. Paul and Clara settled down and, in his spare time, Paul bought old cars and fixed them up. He loved tinkering. Eventually he got a job selling used cars. But Clara missed San Francisco.

In 1952, the couple headed back to

San Francisco, renting an apartment in a neighborhood just south of the Golden Gate Bridge. The only thing missing was children.

A problem pregnancy earlier had ended Clara's chances of having children. The only solution was adoption. Steve was the couple's first child. Two years after Steve joined their lives, the couple adopted a girl. They named her Patty.

Paul and Clara were always open with their children about being adopted. It might have been because people were talking more openly about adoption in the 1950s than they had in the past. As it happened, the first conference on adoption in the United States was held the same year Joanne gave birth to Steve, and new laws to protect adopted children were enacted. When speaking of Paul and Clara, Steve would say, "They were my parents 1,000 percent." In fact, being adopted made Steve feel special:

"Knowing I was adopted may have made me feel more independent, but I have never felt abandoned. I've always felt special. My parents made me feel special."

Paul got a job with a repossession company picking the locks on cars and taking them back from owners who didn't pay their loans. In 1960, the company transferred him to its Palo Alto office in the Santa Clara Valley, south of San Francisco. The family moved to Mountain View, a nearby suburb that was more affordable than Palo Alto.

Shoreline Park, in Mountain View, California. Steve Jobs's family moved to Mountain View from San Francisco in 1960, when Steve's father Paul was transferred to nearby Palo Alto.

Childhood in the Valley

Steve was like most other kids growing up in the suburbs in the 1950s and 1960s. He went to school, played in the neighborhood, and tinkered with electronics. Playing around with electronics was a fascinating hobby kick-started by the scientific research that helped the United States and its allies defeat Germany and Japan in World War II.

Paul continued to buy old cars and transform them inside his garage. He marked off an area to serve as Steve's workbench. Steve liked tagging along when his dad came home from work, changed clothes, and went to the garage to tinker. As Steve later observed, this is where he had his first brush with electronics:

"My dad did not have a deep understanding of electronics, but he'd encountered it a lot in automobiles and other things he would fix. He showed me the rudiments of electronics and I got very interested in that."

Paul was also a perfectionist, and he taught Steve that a job well done extended to a product's hidden parts. In Paul's opinion, even the part of a cupboard that faces the wall, where no one can see, should be built well and look as good as the rest of the cupboard.

Another influence on Steve's sense of building design was the Mountain View house his parents bought. The house was part of a neighborhood influenced by land developer Joseph Eichler. Eichler Homes brought simple, elegant, and affordable homes to the mass market between 1950 and 1974. Eichler's company built about 11,000 homes over that time period. The homes were open and airy. They had floor-to-ceiling glass walls and sliding glass doors everywhere. They had heated floors. Eichler's original design team designed the Jobses' home—some people refer to these houses as "Likelers" because they weren't actually built by Eichler—and it influenced Steve's sense that everyone deserved simple, elegant, and affordable products.

The Jobs's neighborhood also had something that most people don't expect to find in a suburb—a heavy concentration of engineers. Following World War II, the U.S. government continued to spend money on technology for the military. Many companies that did research and invented new technology products settled in the Santa Clara Valley. With so many people and places involved in technology, Steve grew up in the middle of a growing sector, or area, of the nation's economy. Today, with thousands of high-tech companies clustered in this region, the Santa Clara Valley is known worldwide as Silicon Valley.

> *"Life can be much broader once you discover one simple fact, and that is everything around you that you call life was made up by people that were no smarter than you. And you can change it. You can influence it. You can build your own things that other people can use. Once you learn that, you'll never be the same again."*
>
> Steve Jobs

Two views of Santa Clara Valley, before and after the area became better known as Silicon Valley. This was the agricultural region where Steve Jobs was raised among its growing high-tech industries.

Then: A prune orchard in the 1950s, around the time of Steve's birth, when the region was a center of farming in California. Now: The skyline of present-day San Jose, unofficially called the "capital of Silicon Valley." This photo shows the valley's explosive population growth fueled by returning military veterans from World War II and its booming high-tech economy.

The engineers who lived near Steve worked in places such as Stanford University in Palo Alto. Stanford had a cutting-edge electronics lab and had built a business zone, called an industrial park, for technology companies. The Lockheed Missiles and Space Division also set up shop in nearby Sunnyvale and employed 20,000 people by the end of the 1950s. The Westinghouse Electric Corporation, which manufactured missile launchers and other products for the U.S. Department of Defense also moved there. Sunnyvale was also home to NASA's Ames Research Center, where Paul took Steve to see his very first computer. Years later, Steve recalled that he instantly fell in love with it.

School Days

Paul and Clara and their middle-class lifestyle gave Steve an appreciation of hard work and the idea that any job worth doing is worth doing well. But those values didn't always translate into his behavior at school.

Clara had taught Steve to read before he ever walked or biked the four blocks to kindergarten. School bored him from the start. He spent much of the early grades finding ways to drive teachers crazy. Once, with a friend, he made "Bring Your Pet to School Day" posters as a prank. The friends slapped them up around the school, and schoolmates answered the call. It was chaos, with dogs chasing cats and other dogs around the school!

School officials even sent Steve home a number of times. But Steve's parents knew he was a very bright boy, and they believed the teachers should make more of an effort to keep their son engaged. In at least one case, their faith in Steve was rewarded. In the fourth grade, Steve's teacher, nicknamed "Teddy," understood she had an exceptional student. She gave Steve extra work, such as math problems that tickled his brain. At first Teddy bribed him to do the work, presenting him with a giant lollipop and cash. The special attention was eventually enough to inspire Steve to work hard and learn.

At the end of the school year, a test revealed that by the time Steve was ready to enter the fifth grade, he was performing at a high school sophomore level. Teachers advised Clara and Paul to skip their son ahead two grades, but his parents thought one was enough.

"I learned more from her than any other teacher, and if it hadn't been for her I'm sure I would have gone to jail."

Steve Jobs, remembering his fourth grade teacher, "Teddy"

From Cherries to Chips:
A History of Silicon Valley

It's difficult to pinpoint the exact moment Santa Clara Valley, a land of farmers and fruit trees, became Silicon Valley, a land of high-tech computing companies. In 1940, the Valley was still an agricultural center with 100,000 acres of orchards. Farmers grew one third of the state's crop of plums, cherries, pears, and apricots. It was the prune capital of America and one of the nation's top 20 farming counties.

In 1942, the United States plunged into World War II, and all that quickly changed. Local industries switched gears. A company making tractors, for example, began making tanks. Hewlett-Packard (HP) began making electronic equipment for the military. New electronics industries sprouted. Stanford University established a lab that provided electrical engineering know-how and equipment for the military.

The war ended in 1945. Frederick Terman, an official at Stanford, proposed building a high-tech industrial park that would keep the electronics industry centered on Stanford. The park, called the Stanford Industrial Park, opened in 1951. Steve Jobs's mother, Clara, worked as a bookkeeper for the first company to rent space at the park. In 1954, when HP built its headquarters there, it became a center of technology. A year later, seven companies were renting space.

In 1947, physicist William Shockley had created the invention of the century at a research lab in New Jersey. The invention was the transistor. Transistors replaced vacuum tubes, an earlier invention that magnified electronic messages. Transistors did the same thing, but with less electrical

Transistors helped transform radios from large, furniture-sized receivers to devices that were small enough to be held in one's hand. They became wildly popular with school kids stealing a little time to listen to music or a World Series game. Transistor radios (like the one shown right) sold by the billions in the 1950s, 1960s, and 1970s, making them the most popular electronic listening devices ever made.

current and less heat, so they were much smaller. Their first commercial use was in hearing aids in 1952.

Fred Terman wrote to Shockley and asked him to start his own company in Palo Alto. In 1956, Shockley moved to the Valley with eight brilliant engineers to work for him. His company Shockley Semiconductor Laboratory built transistors out of silicon chips, a less expensive material than that used by other companies. The chips are called semiconductors because they conduct, or carry, controlled amounts of electricity.

Unfortunately for Shockley, he was not much of a businessman. People found him hard to work with, and he abandoned the promising silicon transistor project. His engineers believed in the project, however, and bet the future was in these silicon transistors.

In 1957, this group of engineers left Shockley and came to be called the "Traitorous Eight." They formed what is now called a "start-up," or a new company, named Fairchild Semiconductor. The company developed a process where electronic circuits—made up of large numbers of incredibly tiny transistors—could be created on a silicon chip through a process called etching. This meant Fairchild could produce a lot of semiconductors in a short amount of time. The company became a big success.

By 1960, Fred Terman's dream industrial park boasted 32 high-tech companies, and more were coming, spreading out to communities across the Valley. In 1968, two of the Traitorous Eight left Fairchild and formed another start-up, Integrated Electronics Corporation, which they shortened to Intel. Intel developed ways to increase the number of transistors that could be placed on a chip. The result was cheaper chips, cheaper electronics, and eventually personal computers. The semiconductor business could only get bigger, and Intel would soon be leading the charge.

By 1970, the year after Steve Jobs got his summer job working for HP, 70 companies had settled in the Stanford Industrial Park. The January 1971 edition of *Electronic News* launched a series of stories about the Valley's electronics industry and coined a new name for the fruit capital of California. The series was called "Silicon Valley USA."

That same year, Intel shrank the size of features on silicon chips even farther, paving the way for smaller, more powerful computers. They had produced the first microprocessor, the kind that powers most personal computers today, including those made by Steve Jobs's company Apple.

Cherries had made way for silicon chips!

By skipping a grade, Steve ended up in a middle school where he knew no one. He was bullied. He told his parents he would quit school if he couldn't go somewhere else, so Paul and Clara bought a more expensive house in a better neighborhood about 3 miles (5 km) away in Los Altos. The new home meant Steve could go to the Valley's best schools. He began ninth grade at Homestead High School, walking the 15 blocks to school. He enjoyed the time it gave him to think.

Getting into the Electronics Business

When Steve was in his early teens, one of his new neighbors, an engineer, introduced him to the Hewlett-Packard Explorers Club. Hewlett-Packard (HP) was one of the first technology companies in the Santa Clara Valley. In the late 1930s, Dave Packard and Bill Hewlett, two friends and former engineering students at Stanford University in Palo Alto, had started up an electronics company out of Hewlett's garage. They named it Hewlett-Packard (HP). Their first electronic product was a new kind of audio oscillator, a device that helps control sound recordings, and it was a hit. The HP instrument was better and cheaper than what was already available. Walt Disney Studios bought eight to produce the soundtrack for Mickey Mouse's star turn in the 1939 full-length cartoon classic *Fantasia*.

Each Tuesday night in the HP cafeteria, a group of about 15 students met to listen to HP engineers talk about their latest research. At the club, Steve saw his first desktop computer, which he later said was a glorified calculator.

As big and clunky as it was, he fell in love with it, just as he had fallen in love with the first computer he saw at NASA.

In the summer of 1969, before entering tenth grade, Steve ended up working at HP. He had called HP co-founder Bill Hewlett to ask him where he could find a part he needed to complete a project for the club. They chatted for 20 minutes. Hewlett got Steve the parts and a summer job.

Later Steve worked for a large electronics store called Haltek. He learned the value of electronics at the store, which was a huge warehouse where people came to buy and sell parts and other electronics gear. He learned to haggle and bargain over prices with customers and his own manager. On weekends, Steve the budding businessman searched out deals at an electronics flea market, then brought electronics gear back to the store to sell to his manager, who then sold it to customers.

This job, along with a paper route, gave Steve enough money for his first big purchase—a car, at age 15.

"My dad helped me buy and inspect it. The satisfaction of getting paid and saving up for something, that was very exciting," Steve said.

Steve and Steve

One day, Steve cycled over to his friend Bill Fernandez's house. A neighbor was out washing his car, and Bill hustled Steve over to meet him. Bill thought the two would hit it off since they were both nuts about electronics and liked to pull pranks. "Steve, meet Steve," said Bill.

Everyone called Steve Wozniak "Woz."

He was five years older than Steve Jobs and had already graduated from Homestead High, but Bill was right—the two Steves hit it off. They talked for a long time in front of Bill's house about electronics they had designed and pranks they had pulled. They both loved music, and Woz introduced Steve to the music of folk singer Bob Dylan—a singer Steve would admire his whole life. Woz liked Steve. As he wrote years later:

> *"Typically, it was really hard for me to explain to people the kind of design stuff I worked on, but Steve got it right away. And I liked him. He was kind of skinny and wiry and full of energy."*

Steve Jobs (foreground) introduces the new iPad at a tech conference in 2010. Behind him, on a giant screen, is a portrait of him and Steve "Woz" Wozniak (left), taken sometime in the 1970s.

They had similar interests, yet different strengths. Woz was a technically brilliant engineer, while Steve was more tuned into the business and design side of technology. It turned out to be a perfect partnership for transforming the computer industry.

GROWING UP WOZ

The partnership between Steve Jobs and Steve Wozniak paired two kinds of genius. Woz's brilliance in electronics led to the first revolutionary Apple computers, while Steve's creative vision provided the spark for a line of products that have completely transformed the information age.

Some of Steve's early memories were of the time he spent with his dad tinkering with cars and basic electronics. Similarly, the earliest memories of Woz, who was born in 1950, revolved around electronics. His dad Francis (known as Jerry) was an engineer who graduated from the California Institute of Technology, or Caltech. Jerry became a rocket scientist at Lockheed and brought the young Woz to his workplace on weekends. Woz remembers his dad showing him electronic parts and putting them on a table so he could play with them. Woz knew from a young age that he would become some kind of a scientist.

Growing up in the 1950s and 1960s in Sunnyvale, close to Steve's hometown, Woz knew other engineering dads. Like him, many of his neighborhood pals were into electronics. In fact, a group of friends helped him design a house-to-house intercom that connected six houses in the neighborhood. Woz was only about 11 years old at the time.

Woz's parents encouraged his interest in electronics. His dad was a helpful guide when Woz decided to enter science fair competitions with different projects. From the start, he won awards and wowed the adults with his electronic wizardry. By designing and building science projects, Woz learned a valuable lifetime skill. As he once said, "And thanks to all those science projects, I acquired a central ability that was to help me through my entire career: patience."

Chapter 3
The Hippie Years

In 1971, the two Steves got the idea for their first prank together from *Esquire* magazine. Woz read an article about an electronic system that could trick phone companies into completing long-distance calls without having to pay for them. It worked by imitating the tones that telephone routing centers of the era used to automatically connect calls. Woz immediately called his friend after reading the article, and the two pranksters got to work.

"We're Calling You for Free!"

Steve and Woz tracked down a book at the Stanford University library that told them which frequencies they needed to use. First, they tried using a fairly simple tone generator system. It didn't work properly, however, so Woz designed a new digital version. That had never been done before and, thanks to Woz's technical skill, it worked. Their first call was a wrong number, but the two friends were so excited, they shouted into the phone, "We're calling you for free!" They called their gadget a "Blue Box."

After using the first Blue Box to make many prank calls—including one to Vatican City, trying to talk to the Pope—Steve realized that they could sell what they had made. He gathered parts and figured out that each box would cost them about $40 to make, but they could sell it for $150. The combination of Woz's inventiveness with electronics, and Steve's

Steve Jobs gives an onstage presentation at a Macworld convention in San Francisco in 2005.

Steve Jobs (left) and his partner in crime in the "Blue Box" telephone dial-tone caper, Steve Wozniak, are shown here at the unveiling of the Apple II computer in 1977.

ambition and ability to deliver a sales pitch, turned a fun prank into a moneymaking operation.

Selling the blue box took a mix of business sense, electronic wizardry and, most importantly, a willingness to ignore rules and conventions. These qualities would shape the way Steve behaved in life and business. He later said, "If we hadn't made blue boxes, there would have been no Apple."

College and Calligraphy

Steve graduated from high school in 1972. By then, he was already what most people would call a "hippie." He walked around barefoot. He had long hair and a beard. He ate strange foods and read strange books. When he graduated, his parents said he had to attend college, remembering their promise to his biological mother. But Steve didn't really want to go. He told them that if he had to go somewhere, he wanted to go to Reed College in Portland, Oregon. Reed was an expensive school that focused on the arts, not on engineering or electronics. At first his parents said no, but Steve stubbornly said that if he couldn't go to Reed, he wouldn't go anywhere. With that, his parents reluctantly agreed and, in the fall of 1972, he moved to Portland and started taking classes.

The young hippie from California lasted only one semester before dropping out. He was frustrated that he had to take courses that didn't interest him and felt guilty that he was costing his parents money. He knew their finances were already stretched by his stubbornness. But when he dropped out, he didn't want to stop going to school. Instead, he asked for special permission to continue attending classes without being enrolled. Like so many people in Steve's life, the dean of students at Reed College, a man named Jack Dudman, saw something special in Steve. He said yes.

Energized by this new freedom, Steve picked classes that interested him, such as calligraphy. At a famous speech in 2005, Steve said the calligraphy class inspired him to create the fonts, or type designs, that he later pioneered on Apple computers. These fonts are standard on the computers we all use today:

"I learned about serif and sans serif typefaces, about varying the amount of space between different letter combinations, about what makes great typography great. It was beautiful, historical, artistically subtle in a way that science can't capture."

Steve's time in Oregon inspired him in other ways, too. Reed College had a reputation for attracting liberal-minded students. When he arrived, Steve was already a hippie obsessed

ZEN BUDDHISM

Steve Jobs first discovered the philosophies of Zen Buddhism in Oregon, and continued to pursue it throughout his life. What is Zen? The word itself is a clue: *zen* means meditation. The basic idea behind Zen Buddhism is that all the answers to life's questions, such as how to live and be happy, are inside each of us waiting to be found. All the practices of the religion focus on how to look inside ourselves to find peace and happiness. Meditation is a big part of that. Through meditation, Zen Buddhists are able to stop their minds from thinking about the world and start simply experiencing it.

A Japanese Zen monk in a meditative pose in the 1600s. The artist who did this self-portrait also created the calligraphic writing at the top of the painting.

with singer-songwriter Bob Dylan and the counterculture movement. He looked at the world in a way that was different than the mainstream culture of the time. At Reed, he was suddenly exposed to other people who shared his ideas about life. He met Daniel Kottke, a laid-back hippie interested in Eastern religion, including Zen Buddhism.

Steve and Kottke spent a lot of time together meditating and discussing philosophy. They went regularly to a local Zen center, in part because the center gave out free vegetarian meals to attendees. In addition to exploring his spiritual side, Steve also tried what many musicians, artists, writers, and thinkers in the 1960s and 1970s did. He experimented with psychedelic, or mind-altering, drugs and claimed they had a big influence on his creative vision.

Steve never lost his interest in electronics, and Kottke described him as both "cool and high-tech." Hanging out with Kottke and other hippies, Steve spent about a year and a half attending Reed College without paying tuition or getting any credits for his work. He lived in a garage and returned soda bottles for spare change.

Atari and India

After about 18 months in Oregon, Steve moved back to his parents' home and started looking for work. He saw an ad for a job with Atari, a video game company, and went down to their offices wearing sandals and his customary

The upright arcade-style cabinet of a PONG video game stands in a line of arcade games. The Ping-Pong "net" and numbers used for keeping score are on the game's incredibly simple, but incredibly popular, screen display.

ATARI AND PONG

When Nolan Bushnell and Ted Dabney started Atari in 1972, they were looking for a way to make a video game that needed no explanation. The rules had to be simple, and playing it had to be easy enough that anyone could take a turn at it.

The co-founders hired a designer and engineer named Al Alcorn. As a kind of training test, they asked Alcorn to design an arcade game like one they had seen on a new home video game system called Odyssey, by the company Magnavox. It was supposed to be like table tennis, commonly called Ping-Pong. Atari shortened the name to "pong" for its electronic version and sold it as *PONG*. The owners of Atari liked what Alcorn had come up with and decided to try it out at a bar called Andy Capp's Tavern. After a couple of weeks, they were called in to fix the machine. To their astonishment, the game hadn't broken down because of faulty wiring or anything electronic. The problem was simply that it was overflowing with quarters!

PONG went on to become a huge success in the game industry. As simple and basic as it was, especially compared to elaborate video games today, PONG is still praised by some as one of the world's most groundbreaking inventions.

long hair and scruffy beard. The 18-year-old famously told the receptionist that he wouldn't leave until they gave him a job. Luckily, Atari's chief engineer Al Alcorn liked Steve and hired him on the spot. But Steve was a young hippie who smelled bad (he didn't believe in using deodorant) and always spoke his mind, even if what was on his mind was rude. The other employees complained until Nolan Bushnell, Atari's boss, came up with a solution that meant Steve could stay. He told Steve to work the night shift, after everyone else had gone home. Steve didn't mind the arrangement, and the rest of the staff liked it as well!

Atari was a good fit for the rebellious young electronics whiz. It was a casual workplace that held parties and had regular barbeques. But the best part for Steve, and maybe for all of us today, was that the video game company was producing games anyone could play. Their designs were simple and accessible. This was an aesthetic, or set of artistic principles, that Steve had already found in the practices of Zen Buddhism—a philosophy he was passionately embracing in his daily life.

Although the creative conditions at Atari suited Steve, he was restless and eager to continue his philosophical journey. In 1974, he went into Alcorn's office and told him he was quitting Atari to go to India to find his spiritual guru, or master.

Alcorn saw an opportunity to both help Steve out and solve some problems Atari was having. He suggested that Atari could help him with his travel costs by sending him first to Munich, Germany, where Steve would work out some bugs, or flaws, in one of Atari's game systems there. The video game industry was still quite new, and games didn't always work overseas on the first try. Steve, his usual rude and smelly self, offended Atari's German clients—but he did fix their problems.

He arrived in India without really knowing what to expect. His first experience in the hot humid country was getting the intestinal infection dysentery from drinking contaminated water. He lost 40 pounds (18 kilograms) in a week. Feverish and sick, he traveled around the Indian countryside, searching for enlightenment or even just a place that felt comfortable. As he slowly recovered from his illness, he met a variety of interesting characters and holy men, people who spent their entire lives looking for spiritual enlightenment, or understanding. In the foothills of the Himalayan Mountains, he met one guru who shaved off Steve's long hair in a symbolic gesture of health. Later, he met up with his friend Dan Kottke, and the two roamed around the country together for a few months.

Steve was unsettled, and his quest didn't seem to be working out. But one thing had changed. He knew that he had to do things differently.

Back to Work

Back in the United States, almost unrecognizable with his shaved head and new clothing, Steve went in to see Al Alcorn at Atari. "He comes in wearing saffron robes," Alcorn laughed, remembering the scene. "He had a shaved head. He was like Hare Krishna, barefoot, walking about a foot off the ground." When Steve asked if he could have his old job

"That's been one of my mantras— focus and simplicity. Simple can be harder than complex: You have to work hard to get your thinking clean to make it simple. But it's worth it in the end because once you get there, you can move mountains."

Steve Jobs

back, Alcorn said sure and Steve went back to work—still on the night shift. He tracked down his old pal Woz, and the two of them started working on a new video game for Atari. Atari paid Steve, but Woz was doing most of the work. Atari didn't really care as long as the job got done, and Steve and Woz liked working together. Their first big project was called "Breakout," a simple but fun and addictive video game.

As in the past, it was Steve's shrewd business sense paired with Woz's natural ability to engineer clever electronics that allowed their working relationship to flourish. Steve may have been a bit too shrewd, though. He had promised to split the fee with Woz, but he never told him they were given a big bonus for keeping the circuitry simple and compact. Later, Woz said he wished Steve had told him but didn't care about the money. What they were doing together was fun and exciting. That was what mattered.

It was around this time that Woz introduced Steve to the Homebrew Computer Club. This club started informally at potluck dinners, grew to fill a garage, and then finally filled an auditorium in the Stanford Linear Accelerator Center.

It was simply a gathering where like-minded people met and discussed exciting new technologies that were being developed. These people shared circuit schematics, or diagrams, and brainstormed new ideas. They also built working computers. Steve was impressed. Here, there were people like him who not only thought that computers could change the world, but also that the world needed changing. It was the counterculture and hippie movement packaged up in a circuit board!

The Apple Seed

Woz knew how to make groundbreaking circuit boards, but he wanted to give them away for free. Steve, on the other hand, saw a business opportunity. He may have been a hippie, but that didn't stop him from wanting to start a business. He told his friend that instead of showing people how to make their own computers, they should just do the work themselves and sell the finished product. And even if nothing came of their venture, they would still own a business together. Woz agreed. They had a bit of money, a great design, and a plan. But they didn't have a name.

At the time, Steve was still practicing strange diets, sometimes fasting for several days or eating only fruit. The fruit diet was a habit he'd picked up during his time in Oregon, where he worked on an apple farm and commune. When he and Woz were discussing a name for their new company, Steve suggested Apple Computer, Inc. He said that it was fun and it would put them ahead of Atari in the phone book. It stuck. And so, on April 1, 1976, Apple was born.

When it came time to raise money for their new computer business in 1976, Steve and Woz each sold off some of their prized possessions to come up with money to get things started. Steve sold his Volkswagen microbus, and Woz sold his HP-65 calculator, shown here with carrying case and accessories.

Chapter 4
The Rise and Fall of Steve Jobs

Working from Woz's designs, Woz and Steve assembled the first Apple computers in the Jobses' garage. This was the place where Steve's dad Paul had spent years fixing old cars and selling them. Paul got rid of the cars, installed a long workbench, labeled drawers for computer parts, and hung on the wall a big drawing of the computer schematics. Apple computers rolled off the makeshift assembly line. The year 1976 marked the birth of the Apple computer—and the beginning of a revolution in personal computers.

I + II = Apple Inc.

Before Apple, computers had front panels that were hard to read. There was no screen, and no keyboard. Woz described viewing one of these computers as like looking at an airplane cockpit, all lights and switches.

Woz's computer had features no other personal computer had before but they all have featured since—a keyboard and a screen. All anyone needed to make an Apple work was a keyboard and a television. When the computer booted up, users could look at the screen and see immediately what they had input, or typed, on the keyboard. It sounds so simple now.

Not so long ago, the icons that appear on smartphones and computer desktops were unheard of. In the 1980s, two computer giants, Steve Jobs's Apple and Bill Gates's Microsoft, were racing to develop and sell the "point-and-click" technology that we take for granted today.

Steve (left) and Woz work on developing the Apple II computer in Steve's parents' garage, in 1976. The new product was launched a year later, in 1977, at a trade show in San Francisco.

As soon as Woz completed the first Apple (which we now know as the Apple I), he and Steve set to work on the next product, the Apple II. Again, Woz worried about the engineering, and Steve took care of the packaging.

Woz programmed the Apple II to include sound, high-resolution graphics in color, and a way to attach gaming paddles. Steve concerned himself with the Apple II's look and its ease of operation. He wanted to attract everyday computer users to the Apple II, not just serious computer hobbyists. Also, a computer storeowner had told Steve that personal computers should come in complete packages, not just the inside—the circuit board with no outside case, monitor, keyboard, or power supply—as the first Apple was sold.

Steve agreed with the storeowner. If someone could bring a computer home with all the parts and an easy set-up, Apple could capture the home market. Steve wanted the

To See, or Not to See

Although Woz's new computer combined a television screen, or monitor, with a typewriter, it was his HP calculator that inspired the first Apple computer. He realized that calculators were computers, with processors and memories. They also had something else, something that allowed people to use a calculator as soon as they turned it on. This would be huge in the new era of personal computers.

As Woz explained, "When you turned a calculator on, it was ready to go: it had a program in it that started up and then it was ready for you to hit a number. So it booted up automatically and just sat there, waiting for you to tell it to do something."

To develop that for the Apple, Woz created the same kind of programming a calculator had—he used read-only memory (ROM) chips. A ROM chip can only be programmed once, and it keeps its information. ROM chips hold programs that are important for a computer to remember.

Woz created a "monitor" program for the Apple on a ROM chip. As soon as an Apple turned on, the program on the ROM chip would run, telling the computer how to read the keyboard. On June 29, 1975, for the first time in history, people could type characters on a keyboard, and those characters would show up on a screen right before their eyes.

Left: The inside of an Apple II as it would have been presented to customers in its early days. Right: The Apple II packaged and marketed in a way that was closer to Steve Jobs's vision of a product that would appeal to the public. It included (from bottom to top) a case containing the workings of the computer and its keyboard, double disk drives, and a monitor.

Apple II to have a snazzy outside case, a built-in keyboard, software (the programs used by the computer), and a power supply, all in one package. But most of all, Steve wanted it to be insanely great!

Steve insisted on a simple and elegant outside design. He knew what he didn't want—the same clunky gray cases as the other companies produced. Inspiration hit him as he walked by the kitchen appliance aisle at a department store. Cuisinart food processors came in simple, molded plastic cases. That was just what he wanted.

With all these great technical and packaging ideas, the only problem that fledgling Apple Computer faced was money. They needed a lot of it to produce and market the new computer. Steve and Woz offered the Apple II to established companies with money, including Atari. Everyone turned them down, until they found Mike Markkula, a 30-year-old high-tech whiz who had already made a fortune at Intel and had retired. Mike invested $91,000 in cash and $250,000 in credit. He placed a bet on Apple as the leader in a new market—home computers.

Apple was officially incorporated as Apple Computer, Inc., on January 3, 1977.

The Rise of Apple

Steve, only 22, already showed signs that his management style could be harsh, and he had some odd habits. These habits became part of life around Apple's first office, which was a mile (1.6 km) away from Homestead High in Cupertino, California.

To relax, Steve would soak his feet in a toilet bowl and flush. Maybe that was a good thing, as he tended to have dirty feet since he walked around mostly barefoot. Steve was also still convinced that with his vegetarian diet, taking a shower was not required. Michael "Scotty" Scott, Apple's first president, took Steve for a walk one day and explained that his poor hygiene and personal habits made people uncomfortable.

This ad, which appeared in the December 1977 issue of Byte *magazine, portrayed the Apple II as a computer that anyone could operate, with a design that complemented the tastes and lifestyles of people using the machine in the comfort of their homes.*

Steve's drive for perfection, at least with products, also made him impatient and demanding with other people. Getting ready for Apple II's introduction at a computer trade show in 1977, Steve was furious with the plastic cases, which he felt were ugly. He wanted Apple II to look like a high-end stereo system that was popular at the time. At the last minute, Apple employees had to sand, scrape, and repaint the boxes to Steve's liking.

In the end, Steve was right on target. Apple II wowed consumers. Over the next 16 years, the company would sell almost 16 million of the machines, launching the home computer market.

As Apple took off, Steve was in an on-again, off-again relationship with his girlfriend Chrisann Brennan, whom he had met during his final year of high school. She was one of Apple's first employees, assembling the first computer in the Jobses' garage. By the end of the summer of 1977, Chrisann was pregnant with Steve's child, but he would not admit it was his. She eventually left Apple, going back to the apple farm in Oregon. She gave birth to a girl, Lisa Nicole Brennan, on May 17, 1978. It would be several years before Steve admitted to being Lisa's father. When he did, her name became Lisa Brennan-Jobs.

Steve was only 23 by this point. He didn't want to be a father but, in other ways he was maturing. He stopped dabbling in drugs and changed other parts of his behavior and appearance that had been associated with the hippie culture of the 1960s. He began to buy stylish suits and had stylish haircuts. He embraced being a businessman, and focused on

improving the Apple product and brand name.

Though the Apple II was a complete success, it could be better. An annoying characteristic was its ability to only display capital letters in rows that were no longer than 40 characters. The company produced a new computer, the Apple III. Steve designed the computer's outside casing, but it was too small for the components designed by, not Woz, but a committee of engineers. The Apple III never worked as well as its predecessor, the Apple II.

The company needed another winner. Steve turned to another project, called LISA. Although development of the project began in 1978, the year of Lisa Brennan's birth, Steve claimed at the time that "LISA" stood for "Local Integrated Software Architecture." Years later, he admitted that it was named for the daughter he had originally denied. Meanwhile, the Apple LISA computer, like the Apple III, also lacked Woz's engineering genius and Steve grew disappointed with it, too.

In the meantime, the company's fortunes continued to soar despite its problems. One reason was the continuing strength of the Apple

Left: Steve Jobs is shown with his daughter Lisa Brennan-Jobs in February 1989, when Steve was nearly 34 and Lisa was 10. Right: Lisa, shown in 2005 at around the age of 27, is a well-known journalist, magazine writer, and blogger.

II. Another was the educational market. The most popular programming language at the time was BASIC, created by Microsoft. Apple II used BASIC as its programming language. Schools bought Apple II computers and taught students the BASIC programming language to prepare them for the computer age. Millions of students' first experience with computers was through an Apple product.

A Walk in the PARC

While Steve was busy with the Apple III and LISA, another Apple engineer named Jef Raskin was working on an experimental project for the company: a simple, personal computer, as easy to use as a toaster, and costing no more than $1,000. His team of engineers produced a prototype in December 1979. Jef named it after his favorite kind of apple—Macintosh. (Jef misspelled the name of the apple, which is officially "McIntosh.")

Jef knew about a nearby engineering lab run by Xerox, the photocopier company, where the engineers were creating prototype computers with nifty new features. Jef urged his Apple colleagues to visit Xerox. As it happened, Steve was already talking with the Xerox people about allowing them to invest in Apple if they opened their computer lab to him. They agreed to the idea, and Steve visited Xerox at the Palo Alto Research Center (PARC) in December 1979.

As the Xerox engineers were showing off one of their inventions, Steve got up and started to pace. He tried to keep his mouth shut, but he couldn't, and blurted out, "This is insanely great, you're sitting on a gold mine! I can't believe Xerox is not taking advantage of this!"

He was talking about the mouse and computer graphics, things that all computers now have but were mostly unheard of back then.

"It was like a veil being lifted from my eyes," Steve said. "I could see what the future of computing was destined to be."

After the visit, Steve sought out industrial designer Dean Hovey and told him about the mouse. The mouse at PARC, however, wasn't good enough for Steve. Steve explained to Dean how the mouse had to work on a regular desk. Then he sat back on his chair, placed a hand on his jeans and moved it around, adding, "And on my Levis."

Dean listened, nodding in agreement. But when he left to go home he thought, "Is Steve crazy?" Nonetheless, Dean went to a drugstore and bought deodorant that rolled on with a gliding ball at the top. He thought the ball system would work, but he needed a different case. He went to the housewares section of the store and bought a small, rectangular butter dish. The first Apple mouse prototype was born!

Steve was so excited by these developments that he began pouring his attention into LISA, bypassing the project manager

Steve Jobs poses with an Apple II computer in 1981. This was about the time when he and his team at Apple were working around the clock to take user-friendly personal computers yet another leap forward. The result of their labors would be the Macintosh.

and discussing the computer directly with the engineers, sometimes calling them at 2:00 A.M. Steve's behavior was disrupting the LISA team. As a corporation, Apple had a hierarchy, or chain of command, and Steve was not in charge. So the two top Apple bosses, Mike and Scotty, could push Steve into a non-executive position. He remained the face of the company, but now had little power.

It wasn't long before Steve's eye landed on Jef's small Macintosh project. Apple had kept trying to pull the plug on Jef's baby but, each time, Jef managed to convince the bosses to keep backing the Mac team. In Steve, however, Jef met his match. Steve's vision of an "insanely great" product took over. Apple bosses gave Macintosh to Steve, believing that a minor experimental project would keep him occupied. Recalled Steve:

"They wanted to humor me and give me something to do, which was fine. It was like going back to the garage for me. I had my own ragtag team and I was in control."

Steve likened the Macintosh team to a bunch of rebellious and feisty pirates. Not much later, Mike ousted Scotty as Apple president and took over leading the company. He left Steve alone.

The Pirates of Personal Computing

Steve handpicked more people for the Mac team until he had 20 of what he considered A-list, or the most desired, engineers and designers. He wanted Woz's brilliance, but his friend had crashed his airplane, had amnesia, and would be on the mend for a while.

Steve got down to business. He placed the Macintosh team in direct competition with the LISA team, even betting the LISA project leader $5,000 that the Macintosh would roll out of the factory before LISA.

The year was 1981. Who would win?

Steve moved the Mac team to a building near Apple headquarters, near a Texaco gas station. They called their new digs Texaco Towers. In a bid to put his own brand on the computer, Steve tried to rename the project Bicycle. But no one on the team would cooperate, so the name remained Macintosh.

While team members prevailed with the name, they were bowled over by what they called Steve's "Reality Distortion Field." The term comes from a *Star Trek* episode. It meant that to Steve, reality was flexible and he could convince anyone of practically anything, including himself. It was good and bad. It pushed people to do things they thought were impossible. "It was a self-fulfilling distortion," said Mac team member Debi Coleman. "You did the impossible because you didn't realize it was impossible." When something was truly impossible, however, problems erupted. With the Macintosh computer, that meant deadlines were almost never realistic.

Steve had another annoying tendency—an inability, or unwillingness, to filter his thoughts. He was extreme, whether criticizing someone or praising them. "Genius" spewed out of his mouth as easily as "stupid." He understood he could be hurtful. Yet, in his drive for perfection, he seemed unable to control himself. Despite Steve's outbursts, he convinced his team that their goal was his goal: to produce a great product, the best computer ever. They had T-shirts made that read, "90 hours a week and loving it!"

Steve hired two designers to help with the computer's outer casing, but he thought long and hard about it, too. He went back to looking at Cuisinart appliances, and he considered the lines of fancy cars, like a Porsche that he owned. He hung out with Japanese designers, admiring their elegant approach, which reminded him of his training in Zen Buddhism and its attention to simplicity.

The team faced a challenge when Steve walked into a design meeting and flung a telephone book on the table, declaring the Macintosh could be no bigger. He wanted the computer to look friendly, something no one had thought of before. The result was a computer that looked more like a head, tall and narrow, with curved and beveled, or sloped, edges. The competition was short, squat, boxy, and ugly.

Steve also wanted the user to know intuitively, or instinctively, how the Macintosh worked simply by looking at the screen. He focused on the idea of the "desktop" as a metaphor, or symbol, for the computer. This concept was made possible by graphics on the screen. These developments led to new innovative software that would provide the instructions for the computer's operation. Microsoft, a company based in Seattle, worked closely with Steve and the Macintosh team to create the software.

The Microsoft logo. Microsoft and Apple, at times competitors and at other times partners, have long had a "complicated" relationship in the world of personal computers.

Microsoft

Mac vs. Windows

Microsoft founder Bill Gates was, like Steve Jobs, born in 1955 and dropped out of college before becoming another wizard of the computer age. Bill knew the Macintosh was a game changer in personal computing. In fact, he began developing software, later named Windows, for Macintosh's biggest rival, IBM. Steve wanted Macintosh to be the first computer to use icons, and he accused Bill of stealing his ideas. "How could you do this? We trusted you!" Bill was calm. "Well, Steve," he said, "I think there's more than one way of looking at it. I think it's more like we both had this rich neighbor named Xerox and I broke into his house to steal the TV set and found out that you had already stolen it."

Bill Gates, founder of Microsoft, at a technology conference in 2004.

Changes

Everyone was working hard, but deadlines kept getting pushed back. First Steve said the Macintosh would be released in mid-1982. Then later that year. Then the following year.

Around this time, Mike wanted to leave Apple, and the company needed a president. Steve, not yet 30 and more a pirate king than a business executive, knew he wasn't ready for the top job. He recruited the president of PepsiCo, the soft-drink company, to the Apple cause with the now-famous words: "Do you want to sell sugared water for the rest of your life? Or do you want to come with me and change the world?" John Sculley left Pepsi and joined Apple.

The shuffling of bosses meant less to the pirate team at that moment than another big

> *"I don't think I've ever worked so hard on something, but working on Macintosh was the neatest experience of my life. Almost everyone who worked on it will say that. None of us wanted to release it at the end. It was as though we knew that once it was out of our hands, it wouldn't be ours anymore."*
>
> Steve Jobs

announcement—the release of LISA in spring 1983. Steve had lost his bet.

By the fall of 1983, Macintosh was mostly ready. Steve set the price at $1,995. This was the first real disagreement Steve would have with John, who insisted on tacking on $500 to cover the costs of marketing and selling the computer. If Steve wanted a less costly machine, there would be no launch to signal the release of this remarkable new computer. Steve wanted the launch, so John raised the price of the Mactinosh.

That launch in January 1984 was a defining moment for Apple and for Steve. A triumph of marketing, engineering, and design, Macintosh, which quickly became known as the "Mac," convinced John to give Steve more power. He combined the LISA team with the Macintosh team and put Steve in charge. For the next year, Steve became more and more vocal about the way the company should be run, demanding that factory equipment be painted in Apple's bright rainbow color scheme and telling an Apple manager in Italy whom he disliked that he didn't deserve to sell Macs. He was, as one employee said, "completely obnoxious."

By the spring of 1985, with computer sales falling in general, and Steve's disruptive behavior harming the company, he was removed from the Macintosh division. John sidelined Steve.

With nothing to do, Steve sold all but one of his shares in Apple, severing his ties to the company he had founded. He began his post-Apple life with $100 million. What would he do with it?

Steve Jobs (left) with Apple CEO (chief executive officer) John Sculley in January 1984, at the time of the launch of the new Macintosh computer. Over the next year, a power struggle developed between Steve and John over various issues, including management style and falling sales. In 1985, the result would be Steve's leaving the company he had helped start.

Chapter 5
After the Fall

In the summer of 1985, Steve was deeply unhappy. The company he had created with his best friend seven years earlier was pushing him out. There was nothing he could do to stop it. He traveled to Paris with his girlfriend, Tina Redse, a beautiful woman who Steve said was "the first person I was truly in love with." Their relationship was stormy but passionate and, as they stood on the banks of the Seine River, they briefly toyed with the idea of moving to France forever. But Steve knew he wasn't ready to call it quits. True to his feisty and determined nature, he was bitter, angry, and ready for revenge.

> "I feel like somebody just punched me in the stomach and knocked all my wind out. I'm only 30 years old and I want to have a chance to continue creating things. I know I've got at least one more great computer in me. And Apple is not going to give me a chance to do that."
>
> Steve Jobs

Steve Jobs at the 2001 world premiere of the Disney/ Pixar movie Monsters, Inc., *in Hollywood. After Steve left Apple in 1985, he became an investor in Pixar Animation Studios. When Disney bought Pixar in 2006, Steve became Disney's largest single shareholder.*

What Came NeXT

On September 16, 1985, Steve officially left
Apple. He didn't leave empty-handed, though.
As well as the money he got from selling his
shares, he also took with him five top-level
employees. That same day, he created a
new company he called NeXT. It was to be a
computer company that catered to universities.
Apple sued this new company, saying that
Steve and the former Apple employees he took
with him were using insider information. The
battle was featured in prominent newspapers,
magazines, and television shows. Talking to
Newsweek, Steve said: "It is hard to think that
a $2 billion company with 4,300-plus people

*When Steve Jobs (back row, center) was pushed out
of Apple in late 1985, he didn't leave empty-handed.
He immediately got to work, assembling a team of
top-flight co-workers from Apple (shown here). With
Steve, they became the core of his new computer
venture, a company he called NeXT.*

couldn't compete with six people in blue jeans." The lawsuit was later quietly dismissed, and Steve got back to work.

He applied his now-customary approach to management at NeXT. It was the same approach that got him kicked out of Apple. He was ruthless and intense, and he demanded nothing short of incredible results from his employees. It didn't always work. But when it did, Steve somehow inspired the people around him to believe they could achieve the impossible. Unfortunately, it wasn't long before it seemed impossible that NeXT would succeed. Steve was spending too much money on the design and aesthetics, or artistic qualities, of the products and equipment. He even insisted on expensive layout and specific colors for factory equipment—and NeXT still hadn't produced any products. They needed money badly.

Enter Ross Perot, a businessman who would run for U.S. president in 1992 and 1996. Perot felt an instant connection to Steve. He was captivated by what NeXT was trying to do. When the two met and talked about Perot investing in the company, the businessman was eager to get involved. "[Steve] picked himself up, dusted himself off, and started all over again with very little hesitation," Perot said. "And I really admired that...otherwise you could sit around in a dark room and sulk about it, but that's not Steve." Perot's investment of $20 million gave NeXT the financial jumpstart it needed.

What NeXT was so busy designing and producing (and spending vast amounts of money on) was a high-powered computer geared

"Sometimes life hits you in the head with a brick. Don't lose faith."

Steve Jobs

Steve Jobs (left), shown in 1987 with billionaire Texas businessman and future Independent Party candidate for U.S. president Ross Perot. When Steve needed an infusion of money to keep NeXT afloat in its early years, Perot stepped up to the plate to help out. Perot had once reportedly missed out on a chance to become an investor with Bill Gates and Microsoft, and he didn't want to make the same mistake twice by passing on Steve Jobs.

toward higher education. It had lots of unique features, but one in particular had never been done before. It was to have searchable electronic books. This meant that the reader could do a "search" or "find" for specific words or phrases. Steve made a deal to get the rights to the Oxford University Press edition of the complete works of playwright William Shakespeare. He also got one of the NeXT engineers to add in a dictionary. Eventually, they even included the *Oxford Dictionary of Quotations.*

The Point of Pixar

NeXT wasn't the only project Steve got involved with after Apple. He also invested $10 million into a computer animation company owned by *Star Wars* visionary George Lucas. The division of Lucasfilm responsible for computer graphics and animation was on the forefront of using technology for creative purposes. This appealed to Steve, and Lucas needed to sell off the division. The two people who founded and managed the division, Ed Catmull and Alvy Ray Smith, preferred to find investors and keep it part of Lucasfilm, however. Steve wanted the whole package and offered to buy it from Lucas. After negotiations, they worked out a deal where Steve would own 70 percent of the new company, but he had to let Catmull and Smith continue running it. He agreed. They named the new company for one of the division's products, the Pixar Image Computer.

Pixar wasn't just an animation company. It made specialized software and computers for industrial and research programs. Steve had ideas about everything, but it was the animation that captivated him. He connected well with one of the company's employees, John

Steve Jobs poses with John Lasseter (left), head of the creative team at Disney, at the 2010 Academy Awards (Oscars) in Hollywood. While at Pixar, John worked closely with Steve, directed many movies, and oversaw all of Pixar's films as executive producer. When Disney bought Pixar in 2006, he returned to the company that had fired him for encouraging computer animation in the 1980s!

Lasseter. Steve encouraged Lasseter to pursue his interest in creating animated short films that were made entirely on computers. This was something that had never been done before.

Even though they weren't making the company any money, the short films started getting attention. The first one was called *Luxo Jr.* It was a two-minute film about two desk lamps—a parent and a child—pushing a ball back and forth. *Luxo Jr.* was nominated for an Academy Award. It caught the attention of Disney executives, who first tried to get Lasseter to come work for them. But Lasseter was loyal to Steve and Pixar, and he refused. After talks with Steve and the other Pixar executives, the Hollywood giant agreed instead to work with Pixar on producing a full-length computer-animated film about toys. It was to be called *Toy Story.*

Finding Time for Family

While all this was going on, Steve was exploring his personal life. His work on developing Apple products had been so time consuming that he didn't have much energy for relationships. He did have a few flings during his busy time with Apple, including a relationship with the famous folksinger Joan Baez, but these were all short-lived. One relationship—or lack of a relationship—had never left Steve's mind. He wanted to know his biological parents. When his mother Clara passed away in 1986 at the age of 62, Steve felt that he was free to search for his biological mother.

He had already tried looking for her a few years earlier but wasn't successful. Out of respect for Clara, he didn't try very hard. Now, with the blessing of his father Paul, he contacted the doctor who had signed his birth certificate. At first, this didn't get him any closer. The doctor told Steve he didn't have any information for him.

A few months later, Steve received a letter that had this written on the envelope: "To be delivered to Steve Jobs on my death." It was from the doctor, and it contained the key to Steve's search: his biological mother's name. With the help of a detective, he finally tracked her down.

Joanne Schieble, Steve's biological mother, had married his biological father, Abdulfattah John Jandali, shortly after Steve was adopted. They had a daughter together, whom they named Mona. Jandali left a few years later, and Joanne remarried an ice-skating teacher named George Simpson. This marriage didn't last long, but both Joanne and Mona kept the Simpson

Bob Dylan and Joan Baez, shown singing in 1984. In addition to performing together throughout their careers, the two were romantically involved in the 1960s, a time when Steve Jobs became obsessed with the music of Dylan. In the 1980s, Steve and Baez briefly dated and, according to Baez, remained friends even after the relationship ended. She played at Steve's memorial service in 2011.

name. When Steve finally tracked Joanne down in Los Angeles, he contacted her by phone, arranging to meet.

Their reunion was emotional. Joanne apologized endlessly for giving him up for adoption. But Steve reassured her. Part of why he wanted to meet her in the first place was simply to let her know that he was okay with what she had done. At this meeting, Joanne told Steve that he had a sister. Mona was a writer living in New York, and he arranged to meet her as well. They felt an immediate connection, despite not growing up together. Mona wasn't as excited as Steve about discovering she had a sibling but, as they got to know each other, they grew increasingly close. "She's one of my best friends in the world," he said later.

At the time when Steve and Mona first met, she was trying to track down their biological father. But Steve didn't want to have anything to do with this. He himself was also a father who had (at first) abandoned a child. When, in 1978, Steve's high school girlfriend Chrisann Brennan gave birth to a daughter, Steve was

Writer Mona Simpson is shown in her New York City apartment in 1987, around the time when she and her biological brother Steve Jobs met for the first time. Coincidentally, she has both a typewriter and a Macintosh computer on hand for her work!

23—the same age as his biological parents when he was born. His denial that Lisa was his daughter lasted for a couple of years but, when he left Apple, he started spending time with her. He certainly wasn't a dedicated father figure, but he liked the girl who was so obviously his daughter. She was smart, feisty, and outgoing. Steve started taking her on trips with him and spending more time with her.

Shortly after Steve broke up with Tina Redse in 1989, he met a graduate student named Laurene Powell. He was giving a lecture at the Stanford Business School where she was a student. They were seated next to each other while Steve was waiting to be invited on stage, and they hit it off. After the lecture, Steve chased her into the parking lot, where he made a dinner date with her. After turning to leave, he realized he wanted that date right away, so he ran back and convinced her to go out with him that very night.

They dated for about a year before Steve asked her to marry him. She said yes, but it didn't happen right away. Steve could be very intense and passionate, but he could also be cold and distant. He was also confused. He still had strong feelings for Tina, with whom he always felt he had a strong spiritual connection. He asked his friends for their opinions, and his indecision nearly cost him Laurene's love. But she was tough and loved Steve in spite of his personality quirks.

They were finally married on March 18, 1991, in a ceremony conducted by Steve's friend and Zen teacher, Kobun Chino Otogawa. Laurene was already pregnant with their first child.

Back to Business

Meanwhile, NeXT wasn't doing very well. The new computer was exciting at first. For starters, it looked good. The NeXT computer was a 1-foot- (30.5 cm) square black cube made of magnesium. Its nickname quickly became "The Cube." It had cool features such as the searchable dictionary, but a few things made the excitement quickly fizzle out. One thing was its price. The first NeXT computer cost a whopping $6,500. And while it did have interesting features, nothing in the NeXT system could be used with any other software or hardware. Critics considered this a major drawback.

NeXT followed up on this first computer with an even more powerful computer called NeXTcube. Again, it cost too much. The NeXTcube went for $10,000. In 1993, perhaps seeing what was coming, NeXT discontinued its production of computers entirely. The company shifted to work solely on software. Shortly after these changes at NeXT, Steve's father Paul died at the age of 73.

Steve was dividing his time between NeXT and Pixar and his growing family. He had invested more money into Pixar to keep it going, but work on *Toy Story* was slow and not without problems. His financial commitments meant that he was now president and CEO (Chief Executive Officer) of the company. NeXT foundered in the background while Steve focused his energy and attention on the animation studio. But that was about to change.

What's in a Logo?

Steve was always obsessed with image and marketing. When he founded NeXT, one of the first things he did was hire one of the world's best graphic artists to design the company's logo. Paul Rand (1914–1996) was an artist and graphic designer from Brooklyn. His corporate work included designing logos for *Esquire* magazine, UPS, the American Broadcasting Company (ABC), and another computer giant, IBM. When Steve first approached Rand about designing a logo for NeXT, he was told it wasn't allowed because of Rand's contract with IBM. Hearing this, Steve simply phoned IBM and bugged them until they finally gave in.

When Steve met Rand, he told the artist that the NeXT computer would be a cube. Rand said the logo would be a cube as well. But he was insistent about his working conditions. Rand would create the logo, but there would only be one logo from which to choose. No options. No discussion. One fee: $100,000. When he sent his design to Steve two weeks later, he included a booklet that described, explained, and justified his design decisions. Steve liked the booklet so much he had it reprinted and gave it away as a souvenir.

The NeXTcube, with its distinctive shape and cube-shaped logo on its side. With its high-performance capability and even higher-end price, the NeXTcube, like its earlier versions, did not sell particularly well. Most of its sales were to universities, government agencies, and other organizations with many users and large budgets.

The Comeback Kid

Apple was in trouble. The company was losing money and had not released anything worthy of attention for a few years. Microsoft Windows was dominating the software market. This operating system could be used in any PC (personal computer) except the Mac. This meant that Macs had to do something completely amazing that no other personal computer could do, or they had to become compatible, or able to be used, with Windows. They did neither.

Apple needed an operating system like the one NeXT was producing, but more than that, it needed its visionary back again. In 1996, Apple's new CEO Gil Amelio started talks with Steve about purchasing NeXT and using its software for the next generation of Macs. Earlier that year, Steve told *Fortune* magazine,

"If I were running Apple, I would milk the Macintosh for all it's worth—and get busy on the next great thing. The PC wars are over. Done. Microsoft won a long time ago."

It was clear that Steve still had big ideas about the computer industry, even if his own project was failing. Amelio wanted to work with Steve, so they cut a deal. Apple would buy NeXT for $10 a share. The total sale price was $400 million. Steve wanted the deal to include him getting back on Apple's board, but Amelio didn't agree. In those early days, his official title was "advisor to the chairman." It wouldn't matter for long, though, because whatever way you looked at it, Steve was coming back to the company he had created.

PIXAR AND MOORE'S LAW

Gordon E. Moore, co-founder of the computer chip company Intel, wrote an article for *Electronics* magazine in 1965. In it, he predicted that the number of transistors on integrated circuits would double every two years. Integrated circuits are also called *chips* or *microchips* and, basically, they're a way to cram more options, or choices, into smaller spaces. These options include things such as the speed of your computer and its capability to hold memory, where the computer's information is stored. Moore's Law, as his prediction came to be called, meant that every two years, a computer could be made faster, with smaller components, or parts. Since his original description, Moore's Law has proved to be pretty accurate.

Pixar founders Alvy Ray Smith and Ed Catmull knew about Moore's Law when they started in the computer animation business. Even back in the 1970s, they had ideas about animation, but using Moore's Law, they knew their visions couldn't be realized for decades. In the 1980s, their division of Lucasfilm that would eventually become Pixar all but lined up a computer animation film deal. But Smith looked at the figures. "I discovered to my dismay that computers were still too slow," he wrote in an article for *Wired* magazine. "The projected production cost was too high and the computation time way too long. We had to back out of the deal." Catmull and Smith applied Moore's Law and estimated they had to wait another five years before computers would be fast enough for the job. They were right, and their first film, *Toy Story*, was a huge success.

An Osborne Executive portable computer, from 1982. To its lower right sits a 2007 Apple iPhone. The Executive weighs 100 times as much as, and is nearly 500 times larger than, the iPhone. And yet the iPhone has hundreds, if not thousands, of times the computing power of the Executive.

Chapter 6
Back from the Brink

Steve's return to Apple was received with excitement in the world of faithful Mac followers. Of course, not everyone at the company was thrilled to see the cantankerous boss back. But was he the boss? Steve's role at the company as "advisor to the chairman" was initially meant to be informal. But at a Macworld convention in August 1997, the crowd of 5,000 people started chanting his name before he even took the stage. It was clear that the people wanted their charismatic leader back in charge. In his speech that day, he shared his plans for getting Apple back on track. "We have to let go of this notion that for Apple to win, Microsoft has to lose," he said. "We have to embrace a notion that for Apple to win, Apple has to do a really good job."

> "I think we're having fun. I think our customers really like our products. And we're always trying to do better."
>
> Steve Jobs

The underground Apple Store at the Louvre Museum in Paris, France.

The iCEO

Before Steve's triumphant reappearance at Macworld, Apple's board of directors had some important decisions to make. Money was tight. The directors were unhappy with Gil Amelio's performance as CEO. At a shareholder meeting in late 1996, Amelio had to explain why sales had dropped by 30 percent. His pitch was unconvincing. Amelio was a nice guy, but he didn't have the easy-going charm and charisma that Steve could turn on. His presentations were scattered and long-winded. And with the company losing money and the trust of its followers, something needed to change.

Steve Jobs and Bill Gates share a laugh at an interview during a digital conference held in California in 2007. In this photo, they present their two notably different styles—Steve spare and basic in his black turtleneck, jeans, athletic shoes, and round glasses, and Bill slightly rumpled in his open-collar, casual look. Steve and Bill were both competitors and partners, and arguably the two most influential personalities of the information age.

The board talked about it and decided they wanted Amelio out. They wanted Steve to take his place. But Steve said no. He did agree to become a board member, but he didn't want full responsibility of the company. He was CEO of Pixar and happy with his role there. He did, however, want the company he started to succeed and he knew how to do it.

One of the first things he did as advisor was set up a team of people he could trust. He brought his favorite people over from NeXT and set them up in leadership positions. Then he put the Apple employees he had worked with before in similar positions of power. These were all people Steve knew could rise to whatever challenge he gave them. Some of his friends urged him to take over the company by any means necessary, but Steve didn't agree. He was older, he had a family now, and he had plenty on his plate to deal with.

Steve knew that to get back in the game, Apple had to salvage a relationship with its biggest rival, Microsoft. He called up Bill Gates. After talking over the situation, Bill agreed to invest $150 million in Apple. His team would work on making Microsoft software compatible with Apple computers. But when the deal was introduced publicly, via a satellite feed, and Bill Gates's face filled a screen at an Apple conference, the audience booed. They didn't understand what Steve had done. "For Apple to succeed, Microsoft didn't have to fail. Apple just had to remember to be Apple. So I called Bill up and patched things up," Steve said. It took time, but Steve convinced the audience—and later the world—that the partnership between Apple and Microsoft was worth the effort.

Apple CEO Gil Amelio (right) is shown with Apple co-founders Steve Wozniak (left) and Steve Jobs at a Macworld convention in January 1997. This photo was taken shortly after it was announced that Apple would purchase NeXT, bringing Jobs back to the company he had helped start. In July, Apple's board of directors would announce that Amelio was to be dismissed and Jobs would replace him as interim CEO.

He also worked on convincing Apple that they needed to make fewer products. He believed that by creating too many things at once, the company was losing its focus. Steve may have been a billionaire by this point, but he was still the same hippie at heart. He didn't smell bad anymore, but he did still prefer walking around barefoot and wearing jeans rather than suits. He knew that Apple needed to find a way to be simple again, but simply amazing. He started weeding out the products he saw as unnecessary.

When the board finally had had enough and forced Amelio to resign as CEO in July 1997, Steve still resisted taking over the company. He eventually agreed to be an interim CEO—shortened to "iCEO." But, he told the board, they all had to resign as board members, and he would build a new and better board of directors.

It was a gutsy and aggressive move, but the team at Apple didn't have a choice. Steve said that if they didn't resign, he would walk out and never come back. Everyone somehow knew that Steve's visionary genius was the only chance Apple had. They agreed.

Think Different

When Steve was first coming up with a plan for how to rebrand Apple, he called Lee Clow. Lee was the mastermind behind the groundbreaking "1984" ad. Steve wanted to come up with something big, a campaign to "think different," and Lee was the guy for the job. While "1984" was launched to promote the Macintosh, the "Think Different" campaign had no product attached to it. Instead, it was about Apple itself. To Steve, Apple was all about creativity, about changing the world. Lee's team, working closely with Steve, wrote a piece of text that became known as "The Crazy Ones":

"Here's to the crazy ones. The misfits. The rebels. The troublemakers. The round pegs in the square holes. The ones who see things differently. They're not fond of rules. And they have no respect for the status quo. You can quote them, disagree with them, glorify or vilify [badmouth] them. About the only thing you can't do is ignore them. Because they change things. They push the human race forward. And while some may see them as the crazy ones, we see genius. Because the people who are crazy enough to think they can change the world, are the ones who do."

Think different.

The Apple logo as used in the "Think Different" ad campaign, which was launched in 1997 following Steve Jobs's return to Apple. The success of the campaign, along with the return of Steve as the face of Apple, helped restore the strength of the Apple brand. It also laid the groundwork for the hugely successful iMac computer and Apple's leadership in bringing the Internet to personal computers with just a click of a mouse.

The "Think Different" campaign was launched in late 1997. "Think Different" was featured on posters and in television commercials. "The Crazy Ones" was featured in these ads, either in its entirety or in part. In the TV ads, "The Crazy Ones" was spoken by Steve Jobs himself. The campaign was hugely successful and became the key to making the world believe in Apple again.

Lee Clow and his team came up with a visual concept to go along with the text. The posters used pictures of famous people throughout history who had not followed a traditional path in life. People such as physicist Albert Einstein, civil rights leader Martin Luther

The Mac Look

Apple has always been great at marketing, the study and practice of communicating a product's value to people who might buy it. In other words, it's about how to make people want something, even if they don't need it. All of Apple's products and advertisements have a distinctive look and feel to them.

Steve Jobs grew up in the hippie counterculture, and he was inspired by people who rebelled against the "normal" way of doing things. Due largely to these factors, a lot of Apple's marketing has focused on the idea of being different. "Think Different" was just one example of this. Another was called "Get a Mac." Between 2006 and 2009, Apple ran a series of ads that featured two actors, one wearing a suit and the other in casual clothes. They introduce themselves as a Mac (casual) and a PC (suit). Then they talk to the camera and to each other about the different things they do. The script makes the PC appear boring and formal, and the Mac fun and laid back. This kind of marketing makes you want to be the Mac. He's more interesting, the type of guy you'd like to hang out with—which, in turn, will also make you want to buy a Mac!

Marketing campaigns such as "Get a Mac" and "Think Different" are all part of Apple's branding. Even when Apple had yet to capture a huge portion of the personal computer market, one thing stood out: the fierce loyalty of its customers toward the Apple brand. Today, Apple has become a household name with a wide variety of popular devices. One thing hasn't changed: People who own Apple products don't just enjoy using their computers, iPods, or iPhones—they *love* them.

Ever since Steve Jobs rolled out the first Macintosh in 1984, the anticipation over new Apple products has been nearly as much over how they look as what they do. Shown here (top to bottom): the brightly colored iBook G3 "Clamshell" laptop; the Power Mac G4 Cube, with keyboard, mouse, speakers, and Apple Studio Display; and the iMac G4 "Sunflower," with keyboard, mouse, and speakers.

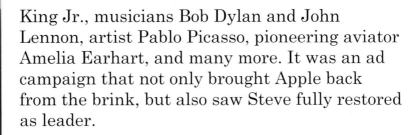
King Jr., musicians Bob Dylan and John Lennon, artist Pablo Picasso, pioneering aviator Amelia Earhart, and many more. It was an ad campaign that not only brought Apple back from the brink, but also saw Steve fully restored as leader.

The iMac

Steve was back, and he was ready to change the world again. At the same time he was working on the "Think Different" campaign, he also started working closely with a young British engineer and designer Jonathan Ive, known to everyone as Jony. Jony had been ready to quit Apple in 1997. But Steve gave his employees a pep talk that caught the designer's attention. "I don't really care that we once had the first successful personal computer," Steve said. "I really don't care that we were famous and successful. We're not anymore and this is where we're starting from and this is where we're moving." He also told them that Apple's goal was not just to make money. Apple was also going to make great products. This was enough to convince Jony Ive to stick around.

Jony Ive, shown here in 2009, has been the lead designer for most of Apple's most popular and groundbreaking products. These include numerous versions of the iMac, MacBook, iPod, iPhone, iPad, and the iOS 7 operating system, which was released in 2013 for iPhones and other Apple mobile listening devices.

Steve and Jony hit it off. As they started working together, it was obvious to both of them that they shared a vision, not only for Apple but also for life in general. They agreed on design principles and approaches to doing business. Steve intentionally set up Jony's position so the designer didn't have a boss, apart from Steve. He invited Jony and his family over to his house, and they ate lunch together regularly. It was a partnership that would have a lasting impact on Apple products.

THE WORLD WIDE WEB

In the late 1980s, a young British computer scientist named Tim Berners-Lee was working for CERN—the European Organization for Nuclear Research. He proposed and developed a project that was supposed to make sharing information between researchers easier. CERN was—and is—a big place, and he wanted to find a way for all the scientists there to work together, without having to physically go anywhere.

The system Berners-Lee developed used something called *hypertext*, which is more commonly known now as "links." When that worked, he had an "Aha!" moment and saw the possibility of making this sharing of information worldwide. He used two other existing technologies to link computers together from all over the world. One was called Transmission Control Protocol/Internet Protocol (TCP/IP), and the other Domain Name Systems (DNS). Said Berners-Lee: "I just had to take the hypertext idea and connect it to the TCP and DNS ideas and—ta-da!—the World Wide Web." Today, the World Wide Web is so much a part of the Internet that it's nearly impossible to imagine going online without using it. Next time you see "www" before the address of a website or web page, think "World Wide Web"!

Tim Berners-Lee, Internet pioneer and inventor of the World Wide Web.

Starting with simple principles that had defined Apple in its early years, Steve came up with an idea for a new computer. It needed to be easy to use. It had to be cheaper than the other computers Apple was selling. And, most importantly of all, it had to look insanely great. That's where Jony came in. He and his team came up with a design that looked futuristic but fun. It had a see-through blue case that let people see the computer chips and circuit boards inside. Steve had always insisted that his engineers spend time making the interior of Apple computers look good. Until now, all that effort was appreciated only by repair technicians. With this new design, everyone could see the beauty that Steve saw. The new computer was called the iMac.

Having a fun, futuristic design wasn't the only thing the new computer had going for it. The little "i" in "iMac" stood for "Internet." One of Steve's biggest strengths was looking forward. He seemed to be able to see what the future of technology would look like before it happened. In 1998, he saw the world changing. Everything was going to be digital. Everything was going to be online. Steve ensured that the iMac could connect to the Internet with just a click of the mouse.

Making all this happen wasn't easy. Jony had to work tirelessly with the engineers to make complicated technology look simple and beautiful. "Our goal is to try to bring a calm and simplicity to what are incredibly complex problems so that you're not aware really of the solution, you're not aware of how hard the problem was that was eventually solved," he later said. And, as usual, Steve set nearly impossible deadlines for the iMac team. As those deadlines approached, he regularly lost his temper. A few weeks before the launch, he almost called the whole thing off because the finished computer had a CD tray instead of a slot. But he backed down from his threats when the team promised him that the next iMac would have a slot.

The new computer was totally different than anything else being made. Apple was going to be the future that Steve could see coming. The iMac was just the first in the "i" line of products that would push Apple to the top of the business world globally. It was funky and functional, and unlike anything else that had ever been made.

The iMac launch took place on May 6, 1998. As usual, Steve wowed the audience with a theatrical unveiling. "It looks like it's from another planet," he said. "A good planet. A planet with better designers." After displaying its many features, the iMac's screen showed the word "hello," written in the same font that the very first Macintosh had used at its launch. This time, in parentheses, a second word was added: "again."

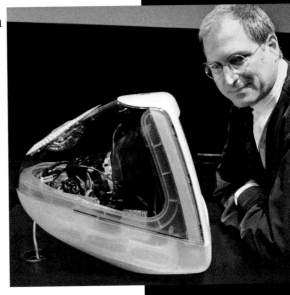

Back at Apple as "iCEO" (interim CEO), Steve Jobs stands next to an iMac in 1999. In addition to featuring a fun, futuristic look on the outside, the iMac's design showed off the inner workings as well. With it, Steve at last achieved his goal of making the beauty of a computer's insides as important as the beauty of its exterior.

Chapter 7
The Man Who Changed the World

The days of the PC, or personal computer, as a self-contained unit with little connection or reach beyond itself, were over. With the success of the iMac came a revolutionary breakthrough into a new market that Steve Jobs was eager to fill. This market was known as cyberspace. In it, the uses of the Internet and other forms of high-speed digital communication were beginning to take flight. At the dawn of the 21st century, Steve seized the moment. He saw a digital future that was no longer limited by circuit boards and buildings. And then he made it happen.

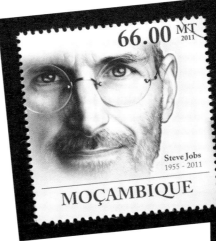

These postage stamps were issued by the African nation of Mozambique after the death of Steve Jobs in 2011. They pay tribute to Steve at various times of his life. They also show him with some of the products he brought into the world, and with various people who shared his vision of the information age.

The Golden Ages of the PC

In January 2001, Steve gave a stirring speech at an annual Macworld convention. Wearing what had become his fashion trademark—jeans, black turtleneck, and round glasses—he strode across the stage and announced:

"I'd like to tell you where we're going. What is our vision? A lot of people have come to ask that about our whole industry in the last few months. What is our vision?"

Steve acknowledged grim predictions that the business of the personal computer was dying. That's not what Apple thought, Steve said: "We think [the PC is] evolving, just like it has since it was invented in 1975 and '76."

The late 1970s, said Steve, was "the prehistoric era ... the early years, [when] no one knew what this thing was going to do." In the early 1980s, new features for the PC were produced and marketed, with Apple leading the way on many of them. These included word processing and desktop publishing. Today we take for granted the ability to write and to produce art, charts, and graphs on computers. At the time, however, these were entirely new. With them, Steve said, "the PC entered what was to become its first golden age...the golden age of productivity," when people could actually create things on their personal computers.

By the mid 1990s, when "people started to wonder, have we solved all the problems that need to be solved with the PC...we entered the second golden age of the PC...this exciting new thing called the Internet."

Steve went on to lay out his vision of the PC's "third great age...the age of digital lifestyle." By this time, digital devices were everywhere: camcorders, digital cameras, handheld organizers, portable listening devices known as MP3 players, cell phones, DVD players, and CD players. In Steve's vision, the Apple Macintosh computer, with its connection to the Internet and growing range of features, was in a perfect position to become the "digital hub" to all these devices. The 21st century was the gateway to this next golden age, and the Mac would usher us through that gateway and to the revolutionary digital lifestyle ahead!

Let There Be Music

While Steve was making this announcement, Apple engineers were working furiously on a new project that involved music. The iMac had a new application to manage music, called iTunes. But transferring music from the computer to an MP3 player was difficult. Steve figured it was time for Apple to develop its own MP3 player.

He called in Jony Ive to design the player. At the time it was code-named P-68, but today we all know it as the iPod. The iPod had a white and stainless steel casing, a flat, rectangular screen, and a scroll wheel. These features, plus the fact that it did not require an on/off switch, made it completely different than any other product. It was the first MP3 player to hold 1,000 songs. Within ten years, over 300 million iPods would be sold.

The iPod was the first "child" of the iMac, and it became one of the first truly personal,

A young woman makes a musical selection on her iPod. Introduced by Steve Jobs in 2001 as a way of extending the iMac's ability to manage iTunes, the iPod has become one of Apple's hottest "i" products

Camcorders and FireWire—The Inspiration for Steve Jobs's "Digital Hub"

In his famous speech at a Macworld convention in 2001, Steve Jobs introduced two terms that became part of Apple's marketing and advertising strategy—"digital lifestyle" and "digital hub." Digital lifestyle described a future in which digital devices and technologies would become more and more a part of the way people led their day-to-day lives. In Steve's vision, the iMac would be the digital hub, or center, of that lifestyle.

The iMac would receive and send information, images, music, and other data, both from the Internet and from other devices, called peripherals, hooked up to it. The iMac also had more storage space than any PCs previously had, with plenty of room to hold files and load new programs, or applications. All this and the ability to provide what Steve called the "horsepower" to operate complex programs, as well as a link to the Internet. The iMac was a natural to become the digital hub connecting people to their digital lifestyle.

Two features that inspired Steve's vision of the PC as a digital hub were camcorders and a system called FireWire.

Portable camcorders (video camera recorders) arrived on the market in the 1980s. Early camcorders needed videocassettes. Within ten years, engineers developed digital camcorders. Apple engineers, with help from other technology companies, invented something they called FireWire, a way to move digital video images from a camcorder to other devices at high speeds.

A young girl uses a camcorder in Rio de Janeiro, Brazil, at a large gathering for children interested in the media.

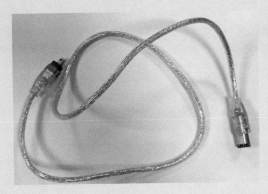

A FireWire cable (left) and a set of FireWire connectors plugged into ports on a Macintosh laptop (right).

Steve realized that with FireWire, people could move videos from their digital cameras to their computers, edit their footage, then share it. So Apple invented the iMovie application. The 1999 iMacs all came with a port, or outlet, for FireWire. At the same time, the price of camcorders dropped from about $4,000 in 1995 to $1,000.

Apple went on to invent other "i" applications that reinforced the iMac's role as a digital hub. These applications included iDVD for burning, or recording, video and music onto a disc; iPhoto for storing and editing photographs; iTunes for managing and buying music. With FireWire, people could send and receive all sorts of new and wonderful things on their PCs!

Photos taken on an iPhone are uploaded into a MacBook Pro computer. In 2001, Steve Jobs declared that "digital cameras now constitute 15 percent of all cameras sold in the U.S.... It'll be 50 percent in a few years." Steve's prediction seemed bold at the time, but it actually fell short of the mark. In just a few more years, digital cameras had pretty much replaced film cameras. Today, film is no longer something most of us would think to look for at a drugstore!

THE APPLE STORE

When Steve Jobs returned to Apple in 1997, one of his first goals was to improve the presence of Apple products in the marketplace. The iMac was drawing more fans to Apple, and the company's online store served increasing numbers of faithful Apple customers. Still, Apple suffered from poor representation in the so-called "big-box" electronics stores. There, customers found poorly stocked shelves and salespersons who had little understanding or appreciation of the Apple brand.

In 1997, Steve tried out an Apple "store within a store" arrangement with the CompUSA chain. Each CompUSA store set aside 15 percent of its space for Mac products and hired a part-time Apple salesperson. Still, customers found little to distinguish the Mac-user experience from that of Windows. Steve decided that in order to satisfy and encourage the customer loyalty that was building up around Mac and the Apple brand, an entirely unique buying "experience" was needed in the retail marketplace.

In 1999, Steve hired a consulting firm to help him put plans in place for stores that would be entirely devoted to Apple products. He also began hiring people with experience in helping other companies, such as The Gap and Nike, design an environment where customers could find the products they wanted and have a great time shopping as well.

The results of this challenge have been spectacular for Apple and its customers. The first two Apple Stores opened on May 19, 2001, in California and Virginia. As of the middle of 2013, more than 400 Apple Stores exist all over the planet.

An article in *The New York Times* described Ron Johnson, one of those people Steve hired in 2000, as someone who "turned the boring computer sales floor into a sleek playroom filled with gadgets." Bolstered by the iPod, iPhone, and iPad, Apple Stores have taken the Apple brand and its message to a larger customer base than Steve and Woz could possibly have imagined when they set up shop in Steve's garage back in 1976.

Most Apple Stores feature a Genius Bar, like this one in SoHo, New York City. Every Apple "Genius" is specially trained to give customers help and tech support for their Apple products.

portable gateways to the Internet. More would follow. But it was the iPod that put Apple at the crest of the digital wave. Because it was so easy to use with an iMac, the iPod drove sales of the computer as well.

Health and Reality

In the late 1990s, Steve had developed kidney stones. This is a condition caused by minerals in the kidneys crystallizing and sticking together to form small hard deposits called "stones." In 2003, Steve seemed healthy, but his doctor thought he should keep tabs on his kidneys and insisted on his getting a checkup. Steve went for a medical scan. His kidneys were fine, but the scan revealed a shadow on his pancreas—a tumor.

Steve had a rare form of pancreatic cancer found in only a few hundred of the 32,000 pancreatic cancers diagnosed in the United States each year. The cancer grows slowly and, if caught early, is often treated successfully through surgery. Steve's cancer was at an early stage. He talked with friends and family, horrifying them all when he eventually decided against surgery.

"I really didn't want them to open up my body," he said, "so I tried to see if a few other things would work."

Like everything Steve did throughout his life, his approach to food was intense. This was no different when he decided to treat himself with a strict vegetarian diet and gallons of fresh carrot and fruit juices.

"Remembering that I'll be dead soon is the most important tool I've ever encountered to help me make the big choices in life. Because almost everything—all external expectations, all pride, all fear of embarrassment or failure—these things just fall away in the face of death, leaving only what is truly important."

Steve Jobs

He also tried alternative treatments, such as acupuncture, herbal medicines, juice fasts, and colon cleansing. Everyone pleaded with him to have the tumor removed.

By July 2004, nine months after Steve's cancer had been diagnosed, the tumor was bigger, and doctors feared the cancer was spreading. Steve finally agreed to surgery and, on July 31, doctors operated and removed the tumor and surrounding tissue. Steve left the hospital a couple of weeks later, so weakened it took him a week to gain the energy to walk around the block. In six months, he got his energy back. There was a chance, however, that he had waited too long and the cancer had spread.

Jobs Back on the Job

Steve went back to work full-time in 2005. He had things to do. Launched in October 2001, the iPod was hugely popular, and the time was right for a follow-up device that would lure consumers farther into the Apple universe.

When the iPod was released, Steve's team had to convince him that to make iTunes truly popular, the iPod should work with PCs that were based on operating systems other than Mac, such as Windows. Allowing an Apple product to be compatible with a computer running a Windows operating system was not an idea Steve cared for. He believed in closed computer systems. This meant that a computer system should not run programs built by other companies. At this point, Apple users could only use Apple products. Windows users could use products produced by different companies, but nothing from Apple.

With the iPod doing so well, Steve relented. He understood that this little music gadget paved the way to the digital future, a future with applications coming from the Internet, not packaged and bought in stores. Within a year of the iPod's release, Apple upgraded it to be compatible with Windows operating systems.

Personal computers, which now included laptops, were certainly around to stay. But as Steve's "digital future" became more and more of a reality, the PC's overwhelming popularity leveled off. On the rise was something Steve had imagined back in the 1980s. It was an elegant, slender computer—a tablet with no

GORILLA GLASS

In kitchens across North America, a CorningWare baking dish probably lurks in a cupboard. Corning Inc., the glass company that created the CorningWare brand, also created the tough glass for the first iPhone, a glass now found in more than 1,000 different high-tech devices.

In the 1960s, Corning had developed a super-strong glass they called "Gorilla Glass." Engineers compress the glass, making it more resistant to bumps and scratches. There was, however, no market for it, and Corning stopped making it. When Steve Jobs started searching for a glass display for the iPhone, he found out about Corning's experimental glass and met with company boss Wendell Weeks. Weeks knew the glass was perfect, but he could not imagine revving up a factory to start making it in large quantities as quickly as Steve needed him to.

Steve turned on his famous "reality distortion field," telling Weeks, "Yes, you can do it. Get your mind around it. You can do it."

In less than six months, Corning had converted one of its factories into a Gorilla Glass factory.

keyboard. It would only need a web browser and a hard drive big enough to store downloaded files and applications, and a screen to read and touch. Jony Ive was working on such a screen. When he showed his idea to Steve, Steve responded, "This is the future."

While Jony had been working on the screen for a tablet-style device, Apple engineers

Two happy customers show their enthusiasm for the new iPhones they have purchased at an Apple Store during the phone's launch in 2007. Six years later, in September 2013, Apple set a new record for first-weekend sales with the release of its iPhone 5C and 5S smartphones—more than 9 million phones sold in a three-day period.

As shown in these two views, Apple TV is a small black box, not a television. Instead of displaying a movie or television show on a computer, smart phone, or tablet, Apple TV streams shows to a TV set. Introduced in 2006, Apple TV connects to a high-definition (HD) television through a cable and connects to the Internet wirelessly. It can also stream music and photos from a computer, iPhone, iPod, or iPad.

were at work, too—on a cell phone that would outshine all the rest. Seeing his engineers struggling to create a stellar display screen, Steve had an idea. He put the tablet on hold and decided that Jony's multi-touch screen would make an Apple cell phone like no other. He was right. The iPhone appeared on the horizon.

At the iPhone launch in January 2007, Steve reminded the audience of two earlier revolutionary products—the first Macintosh in 1984, and the iPod in 2001. The iPhone was even more revolutionary, said Steve. It was an iPod with touch controls, a mobile phone, and an Internet communication device. It was also wildly successful.

Even though it cost a pricey $500, Apple had sold 90 million iPhones by the close of 2010. Apple had half of the globe's mobile phone market.

A Final Act

In 2008, Steve's cancer had spread to his liver, and he was now quite sick. Although he had kept his illness secret for as long as he could, his gaunt appearance worried Apple investors. Steve looked so bad that in June of that year, a news company mistakenly released his obituary (already written, a common practice for famous people). The agency corrected its error, and Steve joked at an Apple event, quoting famous author Mark Twain, "Reports of my death are greatly exaggerated." But the obituary's appearance only increased rumors about Steve's health.

At a Macworld convention in 2008, Steve Jobs introduces the MacBook Air, a new family of super-thin ultraportable notebook computers. By 2008, Steve had become so ill that he began cutting down on his public appearances.

For the next three years, Steve struggled with his cancer. He had always been a fussy eater who was drawn to odd diets where he might eat only one type of food for weeks at a time. The earlier surgery on his pancreas and the cancer treatments made it even more difficult for him to eat balanced meals. He was also in pain. For the first time in 11 years, Steve did not address Apple fans at the January 2009 Macworld conference. He also announced that he would take a medical leave of absence.

At the end of March, Steve had a liver transplant. As sick as he was, he remained his intense, opinionated self, even finding the energy to suggest improvements in the design of the hospital equipment. At one point, he actually ordered members of the hospital staff to bring him five new designs for his oxygen mask!

Receiving a new liver bought Steve some time. At the end of June 2009, he returned to work, and he was truly back in form. He threw some tantrums, told a couple of employees their work was terrible, and shredded some marketing plans. He felt great, ready for the next great product!

Yet again, to the surprise of some, Steve gave consumers something they didn't know they wanted.

Steve and Jony got back to work designing the tablet computer they had set aside while they worked on the iPhone. They played with 20 different model sizes to figure out the best screen size. They designed it with curved corners and a rounded bottom edge that signaled both comfort and strength, a tablet you could grab and go. After the January 2010 launch, not everyone was on board with this new Apple device, called the iPad. Some critics

The Apple A7 microchip is the processor that powers the iPhone and iPad versions released in late 2013. Tiny enough to take up a very modest amount of space inside an iPhone, this mighty little processor holds more than 1 billion transistors. That's a far cry from the earliest transistor radios in the 1950s, which commonly held between four and eight transistors!

Steve Jobs introduces the iPad in 2010.

wondered if it was useful. Here was something that seemed to "fit" somewhere between an iPhone and a laptop. What, they wondered, was the point?

Yet again, to the surprise of some, Steve gave consumers something they didn't know they wanted. The iPad was an easy way to browse the Internet, to access email, even to make a phone call. It held tons of photos. It took photos. It played movies. It was super portable. In less than a month, Apple sold a million iPads—twice as fast as the iPhone after its launch. Both products had the space to accept plenty of new programs, or applications, that provided users with plenty of new things to do. The iPhone and iPad were useful and convenient and, like all Apple products since the Macintosh, they were fun and easy to use. They also helped launch a new industry—creating mobile apps.

As Steve approached the time that would mark the end of his life, it was as though he was in

The iPad has been praised for its ease of use for children in school and home settings. Soon after it was released, it was reported that more than 80 percent of all books downloaded onto iPads were for kids.

a sprint to the finish line. He spent time with family, taking trips to Hawaii and Japan, and surprising his wife Laurene with an anniversary trip to Yosemite National Park, where their marriage took place 20 years before. He was delighted to be alive and in the audience of his son Reed's high school graduation in 2010.

Steve's cancer forced him to take another medical leave early in 2011. In August, he

COMPUTERS? YES, BUT SO MUCH MORE

In 2007, Apple officially ditched the word "computer" from its name. It became Apple Inc. that year, signaling its focus on a larger range of consumer electronics. "The Mac, iPod, Apple TV, and iPhone. Only one of those is a computer," Steve said. "So we're changing the name."

A young woman gets cozy with a collection of high-tech devices, including iPhones, iPads, iPods, and MacBooks. Steve Jobs's legacy includes a revolutionary line of products and ideas for a digital future reaching way beyond the computer. It also includes a huge following of fans who are fiercely loyal to the Apple brand.

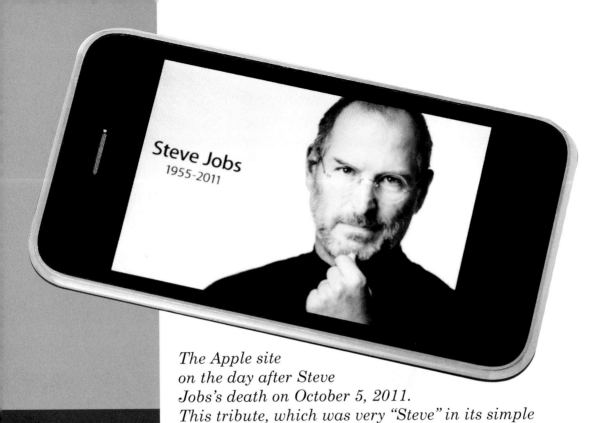

The Apple site on the day after Steve Jobs's death on October 5, 2011. This tribute, which was very "Steve" in its simple elegance, is shown on one of the gifts for which Steve will long be remembered—an iPhone.

> *"Don't let the noise of others' opinions drown out your own inner voice. And most important, have the courage to follow your heart and intuition."*
>
> Steve Jobs

resigned as the head of Apple. On October 5, he died, surrounded by family and friends. His sister Mona, a writer, wrote that her brother's capacity for wonderment remained, even as he lay dying. She recounted Steve's last words before falling unconscious, never to awaken again: "Oh wow. Oh wow. Oh wow."

A Legacy Beyond Measure

Steve Jobs has left a legacy that is hard to measure, because it is so vast. In bringing Apple back from business ruin to a position of supremacy in the computer field, he also brought digital technologies into the homes, offices, lives, and hands of countless ordinary people all over the world.

In his private life and as a business person, Steve had many facets to his personality and character. He was celebrated and adored for his visionary genius, charisma, and passion. He was praised as a leader who could bring people to accomplish things they never thought themselves capable of doing.

Steve Jobs's boyhood in Los Altos, California. It was here, in the garage, that Steve and Woz began making Apple computers in 1976, with help from his sister Patty. After Steve's mom Clara passed away in 1986, his father Paul remarried. When he died in 1993, his second wife, Steve and Patty's stepmother, continued living in the house, which is owned by Patty. In October 2013, the Los Altos Historical Commission named the house a "historic resource." This means it will be protected and preserved as a local historic landmark. The house's new status means that Patty would need to go through extra steps for approval of any changes she might want to make to the house.

> *"Gobble, gobble, gobble, gobble."*
>
> Steve Jobs, mocking a job candidate's long-winded response to a technical question

> *"I guess I'm not the right guy for this job."*
>
> The candidate

> *"I guess you're not. I think this interview is over."*
>
> Steve Jobs

It was also understood that he could be moody, ill-tempered, and harsh. He either loved or hated the ideas that he paid people to bring to him, with little room for compromise. People could be either geniuses or fools. His tendency to see things in black-and-white, with little compromise or "gray" between, carried traces of both inspiration and stubbornness. Each side of his nature could be both a gift and a challenge for those who knew him, worked with him, and loved him. But both were, in their own way, signs of the complex and dynamic personality of Steve Jobs.

Most of us never knew Steve well enough to be affected personally by this inspiring, quirky, and demanding man. Still, he brought richness into our lives in ways that may be difficult to measure, but easy to spot. For nearly all of us, some version or combination of iMacs, iPods, iPads, and iPhones are everyday appliances and household names. Steve Jobs had an almost visionary sense of what people want and need to make their lives fuller and smarter.

The last word Steve uttered might well be what the rest of us are left with when we consider the impact on our lives of this man with the "insanely great" vision: Wow.

Chronology

February 24, 1955 Steve Jobs born in San Francisco, California; Paul and Clara Jobs adopt Steve at birth.

1957 Jobses adopt a baby girl, Patty.

1960 Jobs family moves to Mountain View in Santa Clara County; attends Monta Loma Elementary School.

1967 Family moves to 2066 Crist Drive, Los Altos.

1968 Attends Homestead High School.

1969 Gets summer job with Hewlett-Packard; meets Steve Wozniak.

1972 Steve and Woz begin selling "Blue Boxes"; graduates high school; attends Reed College.

1973 Quits Reed College; sits in on calligraphy class; works for Atari.

1974 Travels to India; stays for 7 months

1975 Arrives back in America; Woz introduces Steve to Homebrew Computer Club; Woz creates the first Apple I prototype.

1976 On April 1, the Apple Computer Company is born.

1977 Apple officially incorporated; Apple II goes on sale; Steve's girlfriend Chrisann Brennan becomes pregnant.

1978 Chrisann gives birth to a daughter Lisa, Steve's first child.

1979 Apple engineer Jef Raskin creates first Macintosh computer prototype; Steve visits Xerox's Palo Alto Research Center (PARC).

1981 Woz crashes his airplane; Steve takes over the Macintosh computer team.

1983 Apple hires John Sculley as CEO of the company.

1984 Famous "1984" Macintosh commercial plays during Superbowl; Macintosh computer launched.

1985 Sculley strips Steve of executive position; Steve quits Apple; cashes in $100 million worth of shares; creates new computer company called NeXT.

1986 Invests in Pixar, a computer animation company; adoptive mother Clara dies; meets his biological mother Joanne Schieble, and his biological sister Mona Simpson.

1989 Meets graduate student Laurene Powell at Stanford Univ.

1991 Marries Laurene at Yosemite National Park; Pixar and Disney make a deal to complete computer-animated movie; Steve and Laurene's first child Reed is born.

1993 Stops selling NeXT computers and begins selling its operating system; adoptive father Paul dies.

1995 Becomes president and CEO of Pixar; Steve and Laurene's second child Erin is born; the world's first fully computer animated movie, *Toy Story*, is released.

1996 Apple buys NeXT for $400 million.

1997 Bill Gates invests $150 million in Apple; Steve becomes interim CEO of Apple; launches the "Think Different" advertising campaign.

1998 Introduces the iMac; Steve and Laurene's third child Eve is born.

1999 Introduces iMovie.

2000 Officially becomes CEO of Apple.

2001 Unveils plans for the iMac as a "digital hub"; opens first Apple retail stores; launches the iPod.

2002 Introduces iPhoto; launches Windows-compatible iPods.

2003 Opens iTunes music store; introduces iTunes for Windows; diagnosed with pancreatic cancer.

2004 Steve's tumor surgically removed.

2005 Gives graduation speech at Stanford University; tells students to "Stay foolish, stay hungry."

2006 Sells Pixar to Disney, a $7.4 billion deal.

2007 Launches iPhone; Apple Computer Inc. becomes Apple Inc.; inducted into California Hall of Fame.

2008 Cancer spreads to Steve's liver.

2009 Takes medical leave of absence from Apple; has liver transplant; goes back to work.

2010 Launches the iPad.

2011 Takes another medical leave of absence from Apple; last public appearance; resigns as Apple's CEO.

October 5, 2011 Steve dies at his home in Palo Alto, California, surrounded by family.

2013 The Los Altos Historical Commission designates Steve's boyhood home, 2066 Crist Drive, of "historical significance."

Glossary

acupuncture A form of Chinese medicine using small needles inserted into the skin to relieve pain and promote healing.

adoptive In a relationship through the process of accepting a child into a family without being related.

aerospace Technology and industry related to air and space flight.

baby boom A large increase in births; the term "baby boom" is most often associated with an increase that followed World War II.

biological Related by blood, as would be a parent who gives birth to a child.

board of directors A group of people who have the power to make important decisions for a company or organization.

cantankerous Grumpy and difficult to deal with.

charismatic Having a special quality that makes people like you.

chip A set of electronic circuits made on one small plate.

Cold War A period between 1945 and 1990 when many countries were hostile with each other but not actively fighting; the two main countries involved were the Soviet Union and the United States.

commune A group of people who live and work together and share their possessions equally.

communist Someone who follows communism, a political system in which ownership of property and money is supposed to be divided equally among everyone.

counterculture A culture that has values and a lifestyle opposite to what is considered normal.

credit Money that is borrowed, usually from a financial institution.

cutting-edge Having to do with the newest and most advanced stage of something, often technology.

cyberspace The environment of computer communications, such as the Internet.

desktop publishing The use of computers to create material that can be read or printed.

digital Related to data processed by using the numbers 0 and 1. Digital devices work faster and store more data than do non-digital devices.

drone Someone who does as he or she is told, without ever asking why.

economy A system of money, often an entire country's system.

electrical engineering The field of science that deals with the study and application of electricity and electronics.

engineer A person who builds or designs engines, structures, or technology such as computers.

font A set of type, or letters and symbols, of a specific style; fonts include styles such as italics and bold.

ground zero The starting point or beginning of a project.

hard drive An important computer part that uses a disk to read and write, or produce, digital information.

high-tech Having or using the most advanced technology.

icon A small image used to represent a file or program on a computer.

invest To give money for the purpose of helping something succeed and hoping to get extra money back when it does.

kick-start To make something happen more quickly.

morality A set of ideas that define the difference between right and wrong.

NASA The National Aeronautics and Space Agency; a branch of the U.S. government that focuses on air and space flight and scientific research.

pancreas A digestive gland located behind the stomach.

prototype The first physical product of a device, usually produced to test for any problems.

share A financial purchase that means one owns a part of a company; when people buy shares, they can then get a portion of the company's profits.

silicon A chemical element that occurs naturally as a sort of crystal or powder; silicon is used to make computer chips because it has natural properties that work well with electronic circuits.

Soviet Union A country that existed between 1922 and 1991 and included present-day independent countries such as Russia and Ukraine.

technology The use of science to make and use machines that have practical benefits.

web browser A type of software used for accessing the Internet.

word processing Creating text on a computer.

World War II A war that took place between 1939 and 1945 and included many countries from around the world, including the United States, Canada, Germany, France, Britain, the Soviet Union, Japan, and many more.

Further Information

Books

Blumenthal, Karen. *Steve Jobs: The Man Who Thought Different*.
New York: Feiwel and Friends, 2012.

Doeden, Matt. *Steve Jobs: Technology Innovator and Apple Genius*.
Minneapolis: Lerner Publications, 2012.

Gregory, Josh. *Steve Jobs*. Danbury, CT: Children's Press, 2013.

Hunter, Nick. *Steve Jobs*. Chicago: Heinemann Library, 2013.

Isaacson, Walter. *Steve Jobs*. New York: Simon & Schuster, 2011.

Lakin, Patricia. *Steve Jobs: Thinking Differently*. New York: Aladdin, 2012.

Videos

Triumph of the Nerds: The Rise of Accidental Empires (DVD/video). Oregon Public Broadcasting/John Gau Productions, 1996. A documentary about personal computer pioneers such as Steve Jobs, Steve Wozniak, and Bill Gates. For a written transcription of the three-part series, go to the PBS website: http://www.pbs.org/nerds/transcript.html

Steve Jobs: One Last Thing (DVD). PBS/Pioneer Productions, 2011. Watch online: http://www.youtube.com/watch?v=SQr0HddYk94. See also the PBS website to read about the documentary: http://www.pbs.org/program/steve-jobs-one-last-thing/

Steve Jobs: The Lost Interview (DVD). Magnolia Home Entertainment, 2012. Watch a preview online: http://www.magpictures.com/stevejobsthelostinterview/. This interview is the full unedited version of the interview with Steve that went into the documentary *Triumph of the Nerds*.

Websites

http://www.computerhistory.org/atchm/steve-jobs/
The Computer History Museum website celebrates the world-changing team of Steve Jobs and Steve Wozniak. The site begins with the pair's joint venture, the telephone "Blue Box"; explains the evolution of Apple; and follows Steve's accomplishments until his death in 2011. Some of the links include the manual for the Apple I computer and the early Macintosh marketing plans.

http://www.ted.com/talks/steve_jobs_how_to_live_before_you_die.html
Steve's commencement speech at Stanford University in 2005, in which he discusses his decision to drop out of college and how this affected the course of his life. He also offers some advice for the newly graduating college students, ending with words borrowed from *The Whole Earth Catalog*, a publication that had inspired him when he was their age: "Stay Hungry. Stay Foolish."

https://www.youtube.com/watch?v=DiGR70BBMt4
Official Steve Jobs biographer Walter Isaacson shares stories about Steve and some of Steve's personal family photos, many of them never seen before, on the television news show *60 Minutes*.

http://www.youtube.com/watch?v=-LUGU0xprUo
Steve and Bill Gates make a rare joint appearance at a technology conference called D5 in 2007. Two journalists from *The Wall Street Journal,* Kara Swisher and Walt Mossberg, talk to the two computer titans for 90 minutes. The interview shows a rare side of Steve as he contemplates the time he has left and his long friendship and rivalry with Bill. The transcript for the interview is here: http://allthingsd.com/20070531/d5-gates-jobs-transcript/

http://www.youtube.com/watch?v=SXSJzWxh0yo
In 2011, Walter Isaacson (Steve's official biographer) spent two hours talking about Steve with the CEO of the Computer History Museum, John Hollar. Isaacson talks about how much better he came to know Steve Jobs after 40 fact-to-face interviews, compared to his other biography subjects, Benjamin Franklin and Albert Einstein.

https://www.youtube.com/watch?v=2zfqw8nhUwA
The famous Apple "1984" Super Bowl ad. Check out other links on this page for views of Steve Jobs introducing the Macintosh computer before "Mac" became a household name.

Index

About the Authors

Jude Isabella is a writer based in southern British Columbia, Canada. She loves digging in the dirt with archaeologists studying the First Americans, and slogging through coastal habitats with biologists studying salmon, bears, and other creatures of the coastal rainforest. Every article she's ever written was composed on a Mac.

Matt J. Simmons is a writer based in northern British Columbia, Canada. He loves exploring big mountains and big ideas, the first with his bike or boots and the second with pen and notebook, and later, his iMac.